Buddha,
Confucius, Christ

Sadakichi Hartmann

Buddha, Confucius, Christ

Three Prophetic Plays

Edited by

HARRY LAWTON and GEORGE KNOX

HERDER AND HERDER

1971
HERDER AND HERDER NEW YORK
232 Madison Avenue, New York 10016

Professional or amateur theatrical groups interested in performing these dramas are asked
to contact Mrs. Wistaria Hartmann' Linton's
agents, Molson-Stanton Associates Agency,
Inc., 9418 Wilshire Boulevard, Beverly Hills,
California 90212.

Contents

Sadakichi Hartmann's *Confucius* is a very beautiful book; and one of those books about which literary discussion appears to me to be useless.

Ezra Pound
TRANSATLANTIC REVIEW, *1924*

. . . positively vicious and salacious according to American ideas.
BOSTON RECORD, *1893*

Mr. Hartmann's *Christ* is a play that defies analysis, and one need hardly say presentation. It is absolutely the most daring of all decadent productions.

James Gibbons Huneker
MUSICAL COURIER, *1895*

Walt Whitman, Mallarmé, Heyse, Brandes, Rossetti were curious what this prodigy would produce. They waited, others waited. Nothing of importance happened. Only the dramas! And they are like unknown vices, they cannot be talked about. Worse, nobody has read them. They are inaccessible. Gigantic in conception like the frescoes of Cornelius and the battle paintings of Vernet, they may yet astound the world when people reassume the habit of studying literature. And again, they may do nothing of the sort.

Edgar Saltus
THE BIBLIO, *1923*

Hugo, Flaubert, Bourget have written nothing that can equal the temptation scene of this poem [*Christ*] in all the nakedness of its abandon.

BOSTON NEWS, *1893*

. . . the author, the publisher, the seller, and the purchaser of C. S. Hartmann's infamous production should alike be adjudged guilty of a crime against the public good, and accorded the punishment due to those who would poison the fountain of purity and truth.

BOSTON HOME JOURNAL, *1893*

You have painted the vast firmament almost as I envision it, decorating the people's palaces of this and future times. The most beautiful aspect is that the colors are those of the dreamworld, delicate and powerful: so that midst the admiration of the crowd, the isolated man also has his exquisite share of joy. Thus the work, as much as by its aspiration, is human by virtue of art.

Stéphane Mallarmé, 1894

It is strange, gaudy, fantastic—a thing all color and incense; something gilded and monstrous and uncouth as the temple of Benares . . . It is vast and visionary. It is not all admirable. At times it is built on black basalt—that black rock of pessimism which is set in the foundations of the world . . . It is a very strong poem. Indeed were it not for a certain frippery of verbal decoration *Buddha* would be in the way of being a masterpiece.

Vance Thompson
MUSICAL COURIER, *1897*

Introduction -

I.

"What's the worst way you could end up?" asks a beat poet in Lawrence Lipton's *The Holy Barbarians,* and then answering recounts his own recurrent nightmare of the artist who throughout life dares starvation and madness for his Muse and fails—"Then I see myself as Maxwell Bodenheim . . . it's horrifying . . . but if it's part of it, if it really is, there's no choice." Maybe no choice existed either for Sadakichi Hartmann (1867–1944), that strange literary figure whose failure surely was more exemplary since he bummed drinks and meals from the down-and-out Bodenheim and slept off hangovers in that ill-fated novelist-poet's Greenwich Village pad. Often called an American Verlaine by admirers, Hartmann began his legendary career in the 1890's as the darling of the American *avant-garde.* His last sick, impoverished years were spent cadging a livelihood off patrons and posturing sardonically before the John Barrymore circle as its clown in rags.

As an impressionable youth in Paris in the 1880's, Hartmann heard the siren's call of Henri Murger's *Scènes de la vie de bohème* and embraced the Romantic tradition's image of the Bohemian dandy as the only role for the creative artist. If he had remained in Paris, Hartmann might have become one of those bizarre *poètes maudits* whose lives are remembered only for their grotesque anti-roles. Instead, he returned to America and became as H. L. Mencken once remarked a "thoroughly American" Bohemian, which perhaps suggests that even as Hartmann roistered through life insulting and mocking Philistines he coveted their applause.

Probably our most formidably intellectual Bohemian, Hartmann possessed an erratic literary talent so undiscriminating that he could express ideas with hammer-like precision and haunting sensibility in one work and lapse into cloying banalities and mawkish prose in the next. Ignored until recently by modern American literary scholarship, Hartmann once had many defenders, including Holger Cahill, who summed him up as "too much of an original for us Americans . . . one of the remarkable singulars who do not fit into our machine life."

Yet Hartmann was eminently American—fiercely so—despite a mixed Japanese-German parentage and a childhood spent on the Continent. Almost from the moment he arrived from Germany as an immigrant boy of thirteen, Hartmann was claimed by the impress of his new land—that vast domain whose free spirit seemed to him to presage the dawn of a native American art. His ideas for his role in that future art, however, were largely influenced by four return voyages he made to Europe between 1885 and 1892. Those journeys brought him into contact with the French symbolist movement and other literary currents, which exerted a powerful effect on his later artistic endeavors and provided models of nonconformity for his own peculiar brand of Bohemianism.

The mildly Bohemian Hartmann of the Mauve Decade was a faint foreshadowing of the unconventional personage of later years. Only with age—as his failures accumulated—did Hartmann fashion himself into a wholly Rabelaisian personality—his own rascally version of the Pierrotic precursor to our Hipster of the twentieth century: the beloved vagabond who lives by his wits and adopts as his aim a life of impossibility, the whitefaced clown of the harlequinades, artificial and spontaneous, heartless and sentimental, irresponsible for his own vices, and master of his own irony. Each failure accentuated the outrageousness of Hartmann's life style. If the world was mad and becoming increasingly madder, as he believed, life could be played out as the cynical charade of a rip-off artist.

It was this "magnificent charlatan"—the self-mocking, rarely serious pose of the aged Hartmann—that Gene Fowler portrayed in his best-selling reminiscences of Sadakichi and his Hollywood drinking companions John Barrymore, W. C. Fields, and John Decker in *Minutes of the Last Meeting* (1954). Behind that harlequin mask, which Fowler captured in bright, amusing strokes, lay the anguished artist, terrified of death and baffled by failure, finding zest only in the pursuit of new sensations. "I'm Sadakichi Hartmann, and I'm so colossal goddam marvelous!" he roared drunkenly one night through the open window of a flat in the Hollywood hills looking down upon Elysian Park. An artist friend, Raymond Brossard, who overheard that alcoholic boast, sensed the frustration and despair behind the old man's outcry. For Hartmann had been defeated—defeated in almost everything he set out to achieve—defeated by the breadth of his many interests, defeated by an inability to discipline and refine his unruly talents, defeated by his own immense vanity and stubborn arrogance, defeated by his too early precocity and far-flung erudition.

Hartmann liked to be ahead of others in his ideas—and then often lost enthusiasm after jumping the first hurdle. He spread his ability over too many genres. He rode his Parnassian horse in all directions, writing one novel, numerous dramas, impressionistic short stories, poetry, social commentary, nature essays, autobiographical sketches, celebrity interviews, dramatic and film criticism, and several books and hundreds of articles in the field of art and photographic criticism. Photographic historians have accorded him a prominent place as one of the more durable and perceptive critics of the Photo-Secession period of American photography, when he ably served Alfred Stieglitz as critical hatchetman in the pages of *Camera Notes* and *Camera Work.* Hartmann's contributions as an indefatigable pathfinder on the frontiers of the modern art movement before World War I have been chronicled by Jerome Mellquist in *The Emergence of an American Art* (1942).

The work that really mattered most to Hartmann, however, was a cyclus of four poetic religious dramas which he wrote between 1889 and 1897 when he was young and waiting for his name to blaze across the literary firmament. The three plays of this series presented here—*Confucius, Buddha,* and *Christ*—represent a remarkable and futile endeavor by Sadakichi Hartmann to challenge and transform the stilted American theatre of the late Victorian period by introducing new approaches borrowed from the French symbolists. Hartmann was heeding a plea voiced in 1885 by Mallarmé for a theatre of myth and irrationality that would transcend the limitations of the well-built play. He was also drawing upon Richard Wagner's notion that the theatre of the future would be a fusion of the arts—poetry and music wedded to mystic elements capable of arousing sensations of awe and mystery in audiences. None of Hartmann's poetic dramas was ever produced—although he and friends gave readings of them in many cities. In an era dominated by the romantic melodrama of Clyde Fitch and the pallid social drama of Bronson Howard, Hartmann's plays proclaiming the absurdity of the human condition were regarded by most readers as the products of a luxuriantly morbid imagination.

Hartmann's dramas have been passed over by modern critics, probably because we wear blinders protecting ourselves from the more self-proselytizing varieties of local literary mavericks. We may explore the legendary scandals of a French *littérateur* such as Hartmann's symbolist contemporary Alfred Jarry, forerunner of the Theatre of the Absurd, who wore a cyclist's costume with pistols, considered drinking a discipline, and puffed and preened hyperbolically. But we prefer our American literary figures to conform to hierarchies established once they are dead. Which is to say strong doses of modesty are expected of minor American authors, and it's safest to be a recluse if one intends to be exhumed. Posturing and inflated egoism are acceptable only in titans such as Whitman and Hemingway.

The curious blend of the sincere and insincere that permeated Hartmann's writings and life have made it easy to overlook him. How much of what he said about himself publicly was true? Did he actually smuggle whiskey to Swinburne at The Pines past the wary eyes of Watts-Dunton? Did he introduce Isadora Duncan to New England, reading passages out of Omar Khayyám as she danced? Was he almost lynched at an art lecture in St. Louis for telling an upper-crust audience that their city had no art? When he reigned as self-appointed King of Bohemia in Greenwich Village was there really a valet who walked before Hartmann to speak to those the master did not deign to acknowledge? Did Charlie Chaplin learn his gestures by studying Hartmann's well-known Delsartean pantomimes and hand-dances? Confronted by the vast apocrypha of tales which circulated around Hartmann and which he encouraged in his gleeful public guise as "The Most Mysterious Man in American Letters." critics who have glanced his direction, such as Van Wyck Brooks, have dismissed him as merely another literary poseur. Ezra Pound knew better and paid homage to Hartmann, speaking of his failure in *The Pisan Cantos,* where he placed Sadakichi at the head of a "lost legion" of American writers of the 1890's, men like Carman, Hovey, Stickney, and Loring, who burned out

swiftly or whose works vanished with the loss of the
fly-by-night periodicals for which they wrote.

Although America's only openly avowed symbolist dra-
matist of the 1890's, Hartmann was not working in total
solitude. Stuart Merrill, whom Hartmann met first in New
York and later saw again in Paris, introduced some of the
French symbolists, including Baudelaire and Mallarmé, to
American readers in his *Pastels in Prose* (1890). Richard
Hovey published a translation of the symbolist plays of the
"Belgian Shakespeare" Maurice Maeterlinck in 1894. Other
native critics, writers, and artists were also absorbing ideas
and techniques from the symbolists. Few of them waded
very deeply into the ash-grey waters of symbolism,
however, and they couldn't always agree on what those
Frenchmen were up to. Hartmann defined symbolism loosely in 1893 as an "endeavor to invest words, by all manner of
expression, with qualities of sound, color, or perfume,"
which got at the movement's roots if not all of its manifesta-
tions and doctrines.

A naturalized citizen, Hartmann hoped to create a bold
new national drama for his adopted country. His concept of
that drama and the seriousness of his effort can best be
illuminated by examining Hartmann's career up to 1897,
discussing his relationship to symbolism here and abroad,
his association with the theatre, and the historical context
in which his plays were written. One fact is worth em-
phasizing: Hartmann threw all of his energies into trying to
become the prophet of symbolism in America. When that
effort failed, he shifted his interests primarily to art and
photographic cricitism. Hartmann's approach to symbolism
was far more militant than that of anyone else in the United
States. Richard Hovey and Bliss Carman borrowed some of
the verbal effects of the French poets, and a more talented
poet, Trumbull Stickney, merged Elizabethan and symbolist elements with elegance and grace. "Take rhetoric and

wring its neck" had been the war cry of Verlaine in his *Art Poétique*. Hartmann got the message and the dramas in this volume were his individualistic response.

II.

Carl Sadakichi Hartmann (Sadakichi roughly translates as "fortunate if constant") was born about 1867 in the international trading settlement on the island of Desima in Nagasaki Harbor. He was the son of an aloof German merchant, Oskar Hartmann, and a Japanese mother, Osada, whose origins remain unknown and who died soon after his birth. Hartmann and an elder brother, Taru, were shipped home to Germany by their roving father to be raised in the wealthy Lutheran household of a Hamburg uncle, Ernst Hartmann, a man of refinement, a gourmet, and a discriminating art collector.

Sadakichi's childhood passed in a cultural mist: years later Hartmann recalled that *dolce far niente* period as a time when he "looked on life as if it were a mechanical theatre." There were regular household excursions to art galleries, museums, concerts, and the toy theatre. Twice weekly during the season, the Hartmanns attended the theatre. By the age of nine, Sadakichi had read *Macbeth* in a Schiller translation, some of Goethe, and a few of Zola's novels. He held magic lantern shows and rigged up paper figures on a wire to stage *Hamlet*. He was so entranced by four heralds trumpeting in the swans at his first attendance of Wagner's *Lohengrin* that he brushed away his grandmother's offer of candy during the performance. In an unfinished autobiography, Hartmann speaks of studying French, English, Latin, and Greek among other subjects in the private schools he attended and learning as much or more by the age of twelve "as any boy who goes through an American high school." His uncle expected him to be able to chat knowledgeably when questioned about art and to differentiate between the quality of various performances of the great German actors and actresses.

The return of Sadakichi's father from overseas and his remarriage to a widow with two young daughters abruptly altered Hartmann's life and shattered the start of a rigorously classical education. The stepmother, who reminded Sadakichi of Strindberg's Laura, resented two boys she considered half-breeds and eventual competitors for their father's inheritance. Taru was apprenticed to a farmer in Holstein. Sadakichi was enrolled in a naval academy to fulfill his father's sudden ambition that he become a sea captain. Hartmann despised the academy's Teutonic discipline; like Wordsworth at Stow he found the hazings by older boys intolerable. One Sunday he ran away to Paris. When Oskar Hartmann caught up with his son, he offered him the choice of returning to the academy or being shipped off to poor relatives in America. In an angry outburst, Hartmann denounced his father and cast his lot with America.

Carrying Diderot's *Paradox of a Comedian* in his luggage, Sadakichi made his way from Ellis Island to Philadelphia in the hot summer of 1882, depressed and appalled by an alien landscape that seemed everywhere to spawn enormous signs for Dr. Schenk's Liver Pills. His aunt, a gaunt old woman in a Mother Hubbard, and his uncle, a greybearded tobacconist, were not overjoyed at the arrival of an odd youth of aristocratic mien in a fancy European wardrobe which the uncle decried as "outrageous." Devoutly religious, goodhearted people—as Hartmann perceived years later—they spent drowsy afternoons in a backyard shooing away flies with palmleaf fans. They couldn't fathom a boy who brought home wagonloads of books which might put foolish ideas into his head. The uncle found Sadakichi a job sweeping floors and cleaning out spittoons for a lithographic firm. At night alone in his room, the boy brooded incessantly over his lost Hamburg childhood; each morning he steeled himself for another day's work as a menial for the sort of people he once considered social inferiors.

Philadelphia was not nearly as provincial as Sadakichi first imagined. He found the Mercantile Library and spent evenings and weekends in ravenous reading—sometimes twenty books a day: Elizabethan literature, biographies of actors, books on dancing, music, Delsarteanism, anthropometry, the fine arts, and the history of the theatre. He tried to familiarize himself with philosophy from Heraclitus and the Stoics to Kant, Hegel, Locke, Fichte, Kierkegaard, Nietzsche, and Bergson. He admired Thomas Eakins' "Crucifixion" at the Pennsylvania Academy of Fine Arts; enrolled in art classes at the Spring Garden Institute where he placed second in a drawing competition; and sought advice on his sketches from the helpful painter Carl Weber, whose woolly sheep grazing against pastoral landscapes impressed him tremendously.

Sadakichi's unusual precocity attracted Dr. Parker Norris, the Shakespearian scholar, and other members of a small literary circle: they allowed the boy to sit in on their gatherings and frequently bought him theatre tickets. Those were the banner years for the American stage. Sadakichi saw Edwin Booth, Lawrence Barrett, Fanny Davenport—even the English actor Sir Henry Irving in *Hamlet* when his troupe came through on an American tour. Often in the moonlight, returning home from the lithographic shop, Sadakichi lingered outside the white mansion of Edwin Forrest, daydreaming of his eventual rise to fame as a dramatic actor and how he would live in that villa.

Hartmann's uncle died when he was about fifteen, his aunt moved in with relatives, and the boy drifted into the streets, working at a succession of odd jobs, pursuing his studies at night. A secondhand bookdealer loaned him a copy of *Leaves of Grass*. When Sadakichi learned that Walt Whitman lived across the river, he eagerly paid a visit to the poet's Camden cottage—the first of many later recorded in his booklet *Conversations with Walt Whitman* (1896). Sometimes Whitman asked Sadakichi to translate correspondence from German admirers; from time to time he made pronouncements on literature and other topics; more frequently he sat bemused by the intense outpourings of the street waif who visited him, occasionally muttering what Sadakichi heard as an enigmatic "Oy! Oy!" Under the spell of Whitman, Hartmann first began writing poetry, painfully derivative, weighted down with such clumsy lines as "Oh, to be a poet, to write with feverish haste, the hand scarce apt to hold the pen words, ideas for ages to come!" During this same period, Sadakichi began publishing essays in the Philadelphia newspapers, some of which Whitman read. Later Whitman told his friend and future Boswell, Horace Traubel, that Hartmann's views "on things Occidental, as they say, are rare, novel—should be heard. . . . Hartmann has written astonishingly good studies. His observations of America are bright—surprisingly searching—some of them."

In the spring of 1885, when he was seventeen, Hartmann raised enough money by selling his library to buy a steerage ticket to Europe to pursue the study of stagecraft in all aspects. His German relatives welcomed him cordially with an understanding that he was now an American cousin. Through the summer, Sadakichi served as a volunteer stage apprentice to the Royal Theatres, Munich. There he assisted the stage machinists, hoisting the evening star over Wolfram-Gura in *Tannhäuser,* pulling Lohengrin's swanboat across the stage, helping produce special lighting effects for the rainbow in the "Dusk of the Gods," and learning to work traps and drops and create lightning crashes by releasing stones down a wooden chute.

He made a special study of *A Midsummer Night's Dream* with the Mendelssohn score, memorizing all the parts, planning to be the first impressario to introduce the work to America. He saw several performances of Ibsen's dramas, and each afternoon on his way to the theatre paused to stare at the great Scandinavian dramatist, who, seated in the Maximilian Cafe, read the newspapers or studied the passing crowd through his spectacles. He watched in awe demons and gods floating in chariots above the stage in the spectacular performances of Kalidasa's fifth-century Sanskrit dramas *Sakuntala* and *Urvashi,* then enjoying a vogue in Europe. He consulted the great German actor Ernst Possart about his chances as an actor. Possart studied the youth—raven black hair topping a high forehead, a long thin nose and pointed chin, and oblique almond eyes—and dashed Sadakichi's hopes by pronouncing such features far too distinctive for anything except character parts.

Sadakichi's disappointment was somewhat offset that fall when he was granted royal dispensation to attend private dress rehearsals for the midnight performances that the mad King Ludwig II of Bavaria indulged himself in about twice yearly. Once Wagner's patron, now living in seclusion, the monarch made immense demands on stagecraft to satify his perverse tastes. Sometimes from his darkened royal box, where he sat alone in an empty theatre, the king would halt a scene to have the actors repeat something that amused him. The aging king, who soon afterwards drowned himself in the Starnbergersee, demanded perfect illusion. The stagehands and electricians, Hartmann recalled in his autobiography, spent many hours of trial and error that year on the royal performance to create a blue grotto with shimmering phosphorescence. The grotto scene—"a huge painting executed in absurd dimensions," Hartmann wrote—featured pretty girls in flesh-colored tights, half-clad in seaweed, against a dark flood of water. "King Ludwig would have loved Hollywood," said Hartmann in his reminiscence.

Hartmann acquired more knowledge of stagecraft on trips abroad in 1886 to London and again in 1887 to Paris, where he frequented the Comédie-Française, watched Cornalba dance at the Folies Bergères, and studied the can-can with Grille d'Egout. All of this training was never used; Sadakichi never was given an opportunity to employ it, but he believed his dramas profited from the experience. He returned to America with euphoric dreams for unusual projects he found impossible to realize.

Between 1887 and 1889, Hartmann concentrated on writing for the Boston and New York newspapers and occasional magazines, while also presenting lectures, hosting concerts, and giving private tutoring in Boston. Most of the *feuilletons* he wrote were based on his European travels and observations on the state of art and literature abroad. Among such essays were articles on current German and French theatre for the *Boston Daily Advertiser* and a vivid review of Mounet-Sully's performance in *Hamlet* at the Comédie-Française, which was published in *Shakespeariana* in 1887.

Impulsively, Sadakichi set out in 1887 to imitate the ubiquitous Browning Societies of that day by organizing a Walt Whitman Society in Boston. Whitman seems to have played along with the idea for a while, curious as to the reception it might meet. Sadakichi was far too young and too removed from the Whitman inner circle, however, to ride roughshod over the poet's older supporters in forming such a society. The project was tabled at its first board meeting, and hung in abeyance for two more years. Finally, in 1889, Hartmann plummeted from grace with the Whitmanites when he published an interview with the poet in the *New York Herald,* which quoted Whitman as comparing the dean

of American critics, E. C. Stedman, to a "sophisticated
dancing master." Whitman needed Stedman's goodwill, and
his disciples urged outright repudiation of the article.
Although Whitman never issued a public denial, he satisfied Stedman by getting word to him through friends that
the statement was fabricated. In 1888, speaking of Hartmann, Whitman had told Traubel: "I have more hopes of
him, more faith in him, than any of the boys." Now he spoke
of his admiring protégé as that "damned Japanee." Yet
Hartmann still continued to visit the poet, and Whitman
never brought up the interview or voiced his displeasure.
Only long afterward, when most of the principals connected
with the affair were dead, did William Sloane Kennedy
voice his opinion that the *Herald* interview was probably
accurate.

Most of Hartmann's energies in this first Boston period,
however, were focused on becoming a producer and playwright. He made plans for an ambitious dramatic season in
Union Hall, highlighted by productions of Ibsen, whom he
later recalled "had just arrived at the stage of symbolism in
The Lady from the Sea." Hartmann wanted to launch three
Ibsen plays that had been translated into English: *Pillars of
Society, The Doll's House,* and *Ghosts.* None of Ibsen's work
had yet been performed in America; a literary columnist on
the *Advertiser* was skeptical of any success, noting that the
playwright's dramas were "but little known here." Among
other dramas scheduled for Hartmann's dramatic season,
which he translated, were Strindberg's *The Father,* Paul
Heyse's *The Death of Don Juan,* Brachvogel's *Narcisse,* and a
dramatization of Hauff's *Othello.* On the basis of promised
backing that never materialized, Hartmann went so far as to
announce opening dates for some of the dramas, including
The Doll's House, and distributed advertising broadsides.

Meanwhile, he was also trying to write melodrama in the
popular tradition of the era and sending his plays off to New

York readers. Only two plays of this period survive: the semi-autobiographical Japanese comedy *Ossada's Revenge* and *Boston Lions,* a rather amusing spoof of Society Lions of the Boston drawing-room lecture circuit. The latter play was loosely modeled on the plot of Kotzebue's *Die Deutschen Kleinstädter* and hinged on a case of mistaken identity. Other lost plays written by Hartmann were *Abraham Lincoln* in five scenes, a one-act sketch called *The Flute Maker,* and *Mademoiselle Bebe,* which required a child lead and sought to capitalize on the success of *Little Lord Fauntleroy.*

After the Ibsen venture failed, Hartmann began giving Delsarte lessons on the language of the body and how to express and conceal emotions. His students were mostly young women fascinated by his rakish good looks, restless energy, and courtly manners. Somehow he discovered the precocious Olive Homans, a clever child of about nine who later became a Hollywood star and leading lady to Tyrone Power. Hartmann decided to cast her in *Mademoiselle Bebe* and succeeded in organizing a company of amateurs and stranded professionals. To publicize the production, Sadakichi held a reception for Olive and another pupil at the Hôtel Vendôme. According to the *Boston Evening Transcript,* almost a thousand spectators mobbed the hotel, where Olive's recitations and Sadakichi's appearance in ornate Japanese robes (rented from a costume house) evoked much interest. Hartmann should have kept his star under wraps. Olive was snatched up by the manager of the Boston Museum stock company and given a lead role in the revival of *Rosedale,* which she helped turn into one of the successes of the season. Whatever backing existed for "Mr. C. Sadakichi Hartmann's Dramatic Season" now evaporated and once more his dreams melted away.

The closest the young dramatist came to being a stage producer of the Gilded Age was about a year later. He collected a troupe of stagestruck amateurs in New York and they gaily set off on a barnstorming tour across the wilds of New Jersey under the name of The Manhattan Company. The play was a Japanese melodrama, probably *Ossada's Revenge,* which Hartmann later confessed had been as serious in intent as an Ibsen work and suffered from all of the faults of a Bowery burlesque. Hartmann's pretty ingénue was a nightwatchman's daughter, naïveté personified, and he was willing to forgive her anything for her "copious wavy hair and her mild and ladylike character." Off-stage she vibrated with the passion of a Mrs. Siddons; before the footlights she delivered lines with the sing-song earnestness of a child asked to recite "The Boy Stood on the Burning Deck." The production bombed in every small town it played in and fell apart in Paterson when the girl's irate father and husky brothers swooped down on the stage and took her home.

Hartmann's first literary efforts in the symbolist genre are a group of poems dated 1887 which make up part of a collection titled *Naked Ghosts.* Several of these prose-poems were privately printed by the author in about 1890 on a broadside of which only two or three copies exist today. Depending upon priority of publication, which has yet to be determined, these poems—actually very poor poems— compete with Stuart Merrill's *Pastels in Prose* as the first published symbolist work in America. Whether Hartmann was in 1887 aware of symbolism as a movement or simply imitating tendencies he had observed in French poetry is unclear.

An article, "Celebrities of the Day: Sadakichi Hartmann, Art Critic," published in *Romance* (June, 1896) refers to Hartmann as "the first prophet of symbolism in America" and asserts that he was writing on this subject as early as 1887. The statement is significant for modern studies into the transmission of symbolist aesthetic doctrines to the Anglo-Saxon world, since scholars generally agree that

George Moore first brought the movement to the attention of the English-speaking world in *Confessions of a Young Man* (1888) and T. S. Perry first used the term "symbolism" in America in his article "The Latest Literary Fashion in France" in *Cosmopolitan* in July, 1892. The term "symbolism" was already current in France during Hartmann's 1887 visit to Paris, having been advanced first in 1886 by the French poet Jean Moréas to describe literary tendencies until then lumped under the label "decadence." If Hartmann upon his return to America in 1887 wrote an article on the symbolist movement, it has not yet been found.

Hartmann was certainly well aware of the existence of the symbolist movement by 1889, however, because in that year he began meeting with a group of young literary aspirants almost daily at the Studio Cafe on Fourth Avenue in New York. This group, Hartmann wrote in his autobiography, included "bitter-sweet Stuart Merrill," whom he respected as a "true poet"; Jonathan Sturgis, a translator of de Maupassant; George Pellow, whose verse has been forgotten; and a youth Hartmann remembered only as McIlvaine, who hoped to become a publisher. Merrill was only four years older than Hartmann but already recognized in France: his reputation as a member of the symbolist movement had been established by the polished craftsmanship of *Les Gamins* (1887); the manuscript proofs of these poems had been sent from New York for correction to René Ghil to whom the volume was dedicated.

On Tuesday evenings, the young men sometimes attended soirées held by the novelist Edgar Fawcett. There Hartmann met the prominent novelist Edgar Saltus, whom he described as a "strange, restless individual with genius written all over him," and his poet brother, Francis Saltus, whose link to an American symbolist current deserves investigation. Hartmann wrote of these gatherings: "The entertainment consisted mainly of conversation and we discussed about all *belles lettres* subjects under the sun. Oh, it meant so much to me to meet these men—their faces, their gestures, even how they dressed, and then, of course, what they had to say, drowsy wisdom and sparking wit, Saltus' cynicism and Merrill's good-humored persiflage. There was also the salon of the Misses Lockwood, some sort of four o'clock teas which I attended various times with Pellew, but bluestockings were not to my taste. I had met too many in Boston."

Over sherry at the afternoon meetings, Hartmann spoke often of a series of prose-poems he planned to write, each depicting a woman's character. He was torn between the title "Pastels in Prose" and "Consolations." Finally, he recalled, Merrill recommended "Constellations" as a better choice. If Hartmann remembered this discussion correctly—and his autobiography accords well with fact wherever it can be checked against other sources—then Merrill's pioneer translations of French poets for American readers owes its title *Pastels in Prose* to Hartmann. (As an amateur artist, it should be noted, Hartmann worked almost exclusively in pastels. An early checklist of pictures which he disposed of shows that he sent a pastel entitled "A Japanese Reminiscence [No. II]" as a gift to Mallarmé in 1894.) Hartmann completed but never published the projected poems he discussed with Merrill. Instead, he incorporated them into the fabric of his first symbolist drama, *Christ* (1893).

In 1890, Merrill left for France permanently, where he and another American expatriate, Francis Vielé-Griffin, became leading figures in French symbolism. The literary circle at the Studio Cafe lost much of its charm for Hartmann after Merrill departed. He moved to the Cafe Manhattan, making it his Bohemian hang-out for the next year, scribbling free-lance articles at tables where he could observe a group of master chess players that included Steinitz.

One day while seated in the cafe, Hartmann read a *feuilleton* by Octave Mirbeau and learned of the new symbolist drama of Maurice Maeterlinck. "What strange visions I entertained," wrote Hartmann, "how I would stage his *L'Intruse* and *Les Aveugles* in a theatre of my own." (The *feuilleton* referred to by Hartmann probably was Mirbeau's "L'Intruse a Nanterre," published in *L'Écho de Paris* on May 26, 1891.)

On the basis of the Mirbeau essay, Hartmann began speculating on the possibility of a poetic drama for America that would employ symbolist techniques. There had been a tradition of poetic drama in America, confined mostly to blank verse, leading exponents of whom were James Nelson Barker, Robert Montgomery Bird, and George Henry Boker. Hartmann was familiar with and admired Boker's *Francesca da Rimini* (1855), which had enjoyed a revival in Philadelphia in 1882 with Otis Skinner in the lead.

If he were to revive that tradition and extend it, what might be his theme? Suddenly Hartmann found himself flooded with thoughts relating to Christ and the sexual temptations that must have confronted him as a young man. Perhaps one of the thoughts brought to mind also was of a nightmare that Hartmann had been disturbed by as a lonely boy in Philadelphia: a German schoolyard, a sandy courtyard filled with dim misty figures, and at its end a life-size figure of Christ on the cross which inspired him with terror; then a terrible shock as if from an earthquake, a blotting out of the stars, and a collapse of the distant mountains in kaleidoscopic fashion with a roar and a rush. Gradually Hartmann's reveries consolidated into a theme for the drama: the battle of eros and agape. The theme represented a compromise with the Lutheran puritanism that was still a predominant part of Hartmann's makeup, which had even prompted him despite increasing agnosticim regularly to attend church in Philadelphia and later to listen to sermons of various faiths in Boston. For several years he had been writing erotic poetry; it was based on sexual fantasies rather than any amatory experience that went beyond numerous mild flirtations. At the same time, Hartmann found himself increasingly attracted to Björnson's ideas on chastity and Tolstoy's views on abstinence. The work that began developing in Hartmann's mind bridged these conflicts. He sat down one morning in 1891 at eleven o'clock and wrote steadily without eating or sleeping until six the next morning. When dawn came, some clothes in his room fluttered suddenly before the wind from an open window. He came out of his trance, shivering, and realized he had completed his *Christ.* There were still minor revisions to be made, however, and several years passed before Hartmann was able to publish the play.

In 1891, Hartmann met and married Elizabeth Blanche Walsh, the beautiful daughter of an English colonel. She brought greater stability to his life, bore him five children, and served as his editor, amanuensis, and agent for many years. Long after he deserted her in about 1910, she still spoke of him with loyalty and affection, once saying: "He was three parts genius and one part devil, and I was in love with all four parts."

In May of 1892, Hartmann persuaded the McClure Syndicate to send him to Europe as a foreign correspondent. The Hartmanns visited relatives in Germany and then settled in Paris from July through October, where their first child, Atma, was baptized on October 6. Hartmann interviewed celebrities, wrote feature articles, and intently prowled the Ile de La Cité, where it seemed to him that all of *fin-de-siècle* art and aspirations hovered in the golden dust that whirled around Notre Dame.

Those exotic figures who were the delight of the boulevardiers fascinated Hartmann. Though the days of the visionary poet Gérard de Nérval, walking a lobster on a leash, were gone, plenty of inheritors of his mantle were to be seen: the eccentric novelist *Sâr* Joséphin Péladan, who paraded the streets in satin garments, hair and beard curled Assyrian fashion, claiming to be an avatar of a Babylonian god; the charlatan Communist Maxime Lisbonne, who drove the city in a carriage moved by electricity, selling "revolutionary" fried potatoes; the *chanteuse* Yvette Guilbert, who sang hauntingly of thieves' dens and the wanton nightlife of the city, her trademark red frizzled hair, black gloves encasing white arms, and a décolleté plunging almost to her waistline; and that most striking personage of all, Paul Verlaine, whom Hartmann described in an essay the following year as "the Villon of the XIX century, an odd mixture of criminal, religious fanatic, and songsmith . . . one of the few who will outlive the literary anarchy of the years 1880–1900." All of these personalities and more Hartmann relished observing and returned to America to write about.

Many of Hartmann's observations of Paris and its literary scene reflect the continuing hold puritanism had upon him. He found it impossible to listen to the languid monotones of Stéphane Mallarmé at one of the poet's Tuesday evening salons without suddenly being thrown back to the dim atmosphere of Boston's Trinity Church, imagining that he was again hearing one of the hypnotic sermons of Reverend Phillip Brooks. Thus Mallarmé, the high priest of symbolism, held forth to his congregation in Hartmann's reveries. Although enchanted by the technical virtuosity of Félicien Rops, whose obscene etchings he first glimpsed in a tiny bookshop near the Bibliothèque Mazarin, Hartmann was repelled upon reading the symbolist poems of Maurice Rollinat, whose *Lés Névroses* conjured up for him all the "stigmata of degeneration." For all his eagerness to embrace the decadence and ally himself with the new schools of literary thought stirring across Europe, Hartmann remained troubled about "those miry depths into which the luring will-o-the-wisp of *fin-de-siècle* art can lead us." If one accepted too seriously the canons of art for art's sake, might not one look into a mirror one morning and see reflected back Huysman's tormented hero, Des Esseintes, or Wilde's anglicized Dorian Gray?

Chatting with his friend Stuart Merrill and other symbolist poets and writers, Hartmann discovered that there was no longer a single school of symbolists, but almost as many sects as practitioners. The movement that had evolved out of tendencies apparent in the poetry of the Parnassians, gaining impetus in a revolt against realism and Parnassian formalism, and crystallizing around Mallarmé and his disciples, now lay fragmented in many schools. Hartmann saw these schools as presaging an unending revolt in the search for new forms of literary expression. Analyzing the development of the movement, Hartmann suggested in *The Art Critic* (November, 1893) that symbolism "was not so much a reaction against naturalism as a chaotic combination of the most antipodal theories of art." Anything and everything was now possible if all literary rules were to be abolished in the *fin-de-siècle.* How far could literary anarchy be carried? Hartmann didn't know, but he was apparently willing to second Jean Richepin who had suggested years earlier that all literary formulas were exhausted and the past should be abandoned. The main thing, Hartmann decided, was to "rush head over heels with new ideas toward the twentieth century . . . [to be] prophets of something (nobody knows what) glorious to come." The inconsistent theories of the past would "be wiped away" and great literary works would no longer be developed from a "certain fundamental idea, supposed 'infallible' by one auguring mind." Thus Hartmann aligned himself with the decadent wing of the symbolist movement—characterized by nihilistic tendencies, existential despair, and a pursuit of the eccentric.

Stuart Merrill thought Hartmann to be pitied for deciding to return to America—that "most inartistic country on earth." Nonetheless, the Hartmanns embarked on the *Gascoygne* for America on about October 22, 1892, and soon after arrival settled in Boston. E. H. Clement, editor of the *Boston Evening Transcript,* recommended Hartmann for an editorial post on *The Weekly Review,* which he admitted might not satisfy his literary ideals but could at least mean permanent employment. Indeed, no duller magazine probably ever existed than *The Weekly Review* as then published by J. Morrison-Fuller. About one column weekly was devoted to literary material, usually cribbed from other sources; the rest of the magazine was simply an exhaustive bibliography of every major article of interest published in America during the week.

Hartmann's effect on the magazine was explosive. Soon after the first of the year, 1893, the magazine expanded to almost triple its former size. Although it published no fiction, it became as volatile and literary as James Gibbons Huneker's renowned *Musical Courier.* Hartmann apparently initiated and clearly wrote most—if not all—of two lively literary columns, "En Passant" and "As You Like It." Innumerable essays, abstracts, fillers, and squibs bear the stamp of his best prose and an encyclopedic interest in everything going on in the world from Aivazowsky's paintings to Zola's ideals on moral education.

Among many pieces attributable to Hartmann are a defense of the nude in art, which featured the magazine's first use of photographic illustration; a campaign to preserve Whitman's Camden cottage and a rewrite of Hartmann's *Herald* interview with the poet; theatrical gossip on Eleonora Duse, Yvette Guilbert, and André Antoine's Théâtre Libre and Lugné-Poë's symbolist Théâtre d'Art of Paris; commentary on Sardou's plays, Bernard Shaw's views on Ibsen, Mayrrhoffer's transparent scenery and exotic lighting effects, and dramatic art in Iceland; and discussions of symbolism ranging from analysis of the scientific basis of Rimbaud's association of colors and sound to the waspish suggestion that Aline Gorren's pioneer essay on "The French Symbolists" in *Scribner's* (January-June, 1893) was about a decade too late if she imagined herself on to the latest literary fashion.

Perhaps the magazine grew too fast to pace circulation; maybe Morrison-Fuller got wind of the fact that Hartmann was considering publishing his own magazine. In any event, *The Weekly Review* folded without explanation on April 29, 1893, after about twenty first-rate issues crammed with Hartmann contributions.

Hartmann's activities in Boston during his tenure on *The Weekly Review* were not confined to his editorial tasks. He continued writing symbolist poetry of a lush, flowery sort. One of these poems, "A Strain in Red," dated 1892, was dedicated to Mallarmé as was his unpublished collection *Naked Ghosts* (1898). He also wrote essays on a variety of topics for other publications, including a long article on Antoine's Théâtre Libre for the *Transcript*. He recalled first encountering Vance Thompson, whose *French Portraits* (1900) provided Americans with an anecdotal chronicle of the symbolist movement, while attending Yvette Guilbert's New York debut. Richard Hovey came up from New York to organize a branch of the Theatre of Arts and Letters in Boston. Hartmann was a subscribing member of this organization, attending most of its productions and other major Boston stage presentations as well. He made friends with a leading American actress of the day, Sadie Martinot, who tried to get some of his melodramas produced and served as a godmother for one of his children.

Some time in the spring of 1893, Hartmann began checking proofs for his first published drama, *Christ*. The play was advertised in *The Weekly Review* on April 15, and privately released by its author in an edition of about 1020 copies in May. There were several news stories about its publication in the Boston papers, but it appears to have attracted little notice for a number of months. Meanwhile, Hartmann plunged ahead on composition of his second symbolist drama, *Buddha,* first begun in 1891, which was to be his "scarlet departure." In reading the lyrical *Christ,* one is somewhat reminded of Maeterlinck's *Pelléas et Mélisande,* which opened in Paris in the same month that Hartmann's play was published. With *Buddha,* however, Hartmann abandoned most of the conventions tying symbolist drama to the past, including the historical surface naturalism of *Christ.* Although *Buddha* in no way parallels Kalidasa's *Sakuntala,* some of the exotic atmosphere and scenic effects can probably be ascribed to Hartmann's remembrance of that early Sanskrit drama he saw staged in Munich in 1885.

In the summer of 1893, Hartmann traveled up and down New England with a prospectus for his own literary and art magazine, *The Art Critic.* He visited several hundred artist's studios, seeking support and taking advance orders from 388 subscribers. *Kate Field's Washington* praised the magazine's announced goal of enlisting government support for American art and artists. Hartmann's subscription list included most of the current giants of American art— Augustus St. Gaudens, Thomas W. Dewing, and Albert Bierstadt—and a roster of names scarcely known to the public for another decade, among them Robert Henri, Arthur B. Davies, and Albert Pinkham Ryder. Sadakichi hurled himself into the project with gusto, visiting art exhibitions and writing reviews, denouncing the provincialism of art in Boston, turning out short stories and leisurely essays, and bearding artists in their studios for firsthand interviews on technique. Elizabeth helped with editing and layout, and E. B. Bird designed a rococco cover with a cherub holding an artist's pallette. The first issue of the bi-monthly appeared in November, 1893.

Essentially, the magazine was an organ for symbolist ideas, although Hartmann often used the phrase *"fin-de-siècle* art." In the first number, he issued a manifesto, "What is Fin De Siècle?" It was a call to American artists and writers to reject the past and "go from darkness to light, from light to darkness, and again, to light, to the light of lights." Both from America and abroad came letters from subscribers with lavish praise for the new magazine.

Elizabeth was constantly forced to nag her husband about the business end of the venture, pressing him to drum up more advertising and dun subscribers who were tardy in payments. Hartmann's attention was fixed only on the journal's contents, however, and he wrote the bulk of each of the three issues published. Among Hartmann's many contributions to the magazine were a plea for the establishment of a National Gallery of Art; an analysis of symbolist painters, including possibly the earliest mention of Gauguin in America; an account of a Tuesday evening with Stéphane Mallarmé; a translation of *Sâr* Péladan's catalogue for the 1892 exhibition of symbolist artists at the Salon de la Rose-Croix; an evaluation of the painter Puvis de Chavannes; and a discussion of American literature that saw Henry James as one of the "forerunners of the great novel and great drama America needs."

The unusual views expressed in *The Art Critic,* where one might learn of the existence of an infamous Marquis de Sade or that certain women at the Chat Noir in Paris danced with skirts too high, may have attracted undue attention to the strange young editor in Boston's midst. The *Boston Record* suddenly got around to examining his drama *Christ* and discovered it was "vicious and salacious according to American ideas." The newspaper launched a crusade demanding confiscation of the book. The New England Watch and Ward Society finally swung into action. On December 21, 1893, all copies of *Christ* were seized and Hartmann was arrested on obscenity charges and thrown into Charles Street Jail. He spent Christmas week in jail, remaining there until January 2 when three local artists, J. T. S. Monks, F. H. Thompkins, and F. W. Henwood went his $500 bail.

In February, 1894, unwilling to create hardship for his wife and children, Hartmann pleaded guilty to the charge. Attorney Timothy W. Coakley delivered a "splendid plea" for leniency and the Superior Court Judge fined Hartmann only $100. Most of the printing of *Christ*, except for a few copies that had been sold in this country and several hundred that had been sent to Europe, were destroyed. Because many subscriptions had not been paid, advertising had been neglected, and the costs of his arrest and trial had wiped Hartmann out financially, he was forced to suspend publication of his magazine with the issue of March, 1894. In the last issue, he defended free speech in literature and swore: "Henceforth my future works of this character will be published in Paris." With that promise, which he failed to keep, Hartmann moved to New York, where for the next few years he wrote freelance articles, served on several magazine staffs, and worked to complete the three remaining dramas of his religious cyclus: *Buddha, Confucius,* and *Mohammed.*

Hartmann's connections with symbolism continued to be evidenced in his writings, personal associations, and correspondence up until 1899, when he wrote an essay on the symbolist poet Henri de Régnier for the *New Yorker Staats-Zeitung.* His impressionistic short-story collection *Schopenhauer in the Air* (1899) contains a story called "The Wife of the Symbolist." He helped the American symbolist poet Anne Throop publish her *Whisperings of a Windharp* (1897), and wrote an introduction. He corresponded with symbolists abroad, among them Mallarmé and Rémy de Gour-mont, whose letters to Hartmann have not been seen since about 1915 when they were sold by Breslow's Bookshop in New York. Mentions of symbolism also crop up in a small, cheaply printed magazine, *Art News,* which Hartmann tried to get going in New York in 1897, although this publication lacks the air of excitement over symbolism and the ty-pographical quality that characterized his first magazine.

Among Hartmann's papers is a list of projects marked "Schemes," containing a plan for a cafe to have been called "The Mecca: Café Intime and Hangout of Symbolism." Membership in the cafe's salon would have followed the order of *Sâr* Péladan's esoteric Rosicrucian cult with Hart-mann serving as "Innkeeper and Poet," Albert Pinkham Ryder as "Grand Prior," and other writers and poets filling the posts of "Tetrarchs," "Archons," and "Doctors of Art." The projected cafe (1893-1896?) may have been only a daydream or a bit of drollery dashed off to amuse friends. There is also Hartmann's chapter-by-chapter outline for a book, *Modern French Symbolists,* which would have covered major figures and schools of the movement and focused also on artists such as Odilon Redon and Félicien Rops. A third project—possibly an annual or anthology—would have brought together essays by Aline Gorren, Stuart Merrill, Jonathan Sturgis, James Gibbons Huneker, Dempster Sher-man, Ralph Adams Cram, and Bliss Carman—all of whom are linked by some degree of interest in symbolism.

Hartmann's actual literary endeavors as a symbolist can be said to have reached a culmination in 1896, coinciding with the flickering twilight of the movement from that year on in France. He completed *Buddha* in 1895, publishing it in 1897. *Confucius* was essentially finished when Hartmann gave his first reading of it at the studio of Edmund Russell, the actor, in 1896. He was unable to publish it, however, until 1923 when Douglas Fairbanks hired him at an exorbitant salary to play the role of court magician in *The Thief of Bagdad.* Also completed in 1896 was *Mohammed,* which rounded out Hartmann's planned religious cyclus and which remains unpublished. Two later dramas, *Moses* (1934) and *Baker Eddy* (1938), are products of Hartmann's old age when his thoughts turned back with increasing nostalgia to the Mauve Decade and he regretted that the "reign of symbolism was of short durance."

Although Hartmann's effort to introduce a new American drama was unsuccessful, his plays received some attention at the time. A number of American and European reviewers recognized that he was working in the symbolist mode. Vance Thompson praised *Buddha* as "strange, gaudy, fantastic—a thing all color and incense; something as gilded and monstrous and uncouth as the temple of Benares." James Gibbons Huneker admitted that there was "no denying the merits of *Buddha* and *Christ,*" but argued they were not plays for the public and were "united to a mode of thought that would jail the poet-dramatist if his works ever got before the footlights." The critic E. C. Stedman wrote Hartmann begging him to try his hand at plays "this side the borderline." Stedman added: "You are too cosmic and various and must get hold of the time and place of your fellow beings." Frederick Dana Marsh, the American muralist, studying in Europe in 1894, wrote Hartmann, whom he addressed as "My dear Symbolist" to say he was passing on copies of *Christ* to Whistler and Sargent. Stéphane Mallarmé read *Christ* and responded:

Thank you for sending me Christ, my dear poet; with regret for so tardy a word. You have painted the vast firmament almost as I envision it, decorating the people's palaces of this and future times. The most beautiful aspect is that the colors are those of the dreamworld, delicate and powerful; so that midst the admiration of the crowd, the isolated man also has his exquisite share of joy.

Thus the work, as much as by its aspirations, is human by virtue of art.

Your hand,
[Stéphane Mallarmé]

From his first symbolist play, *Christ,* which still observed the pyramidal construction of the well-built play, Hartmann moved forward in the three later dramas to construct a radically innovative theatre. In their savage humor, episodic structure, and emphasis upon the absurd, Hartmann's later dramas bear comparison with Alfred Jarry's *Ubu Roi,* which satirizes the evil in man by presenting a phantasmagoric kingdom dominated by the merciless King Ubu. Both Jarry's dramas and Hartmann's have much in common in their exploration of the margins of reality.

If 1896 marked the end of Hartmann's attempts to establish a symbolist drama in America, one is reminded that the same year saw Jarry's *Ubu Roi* staged by Lugné-Poë on the night of December 10 in the Théâtre de l'Oeuvre in Paris. There was pandemonium and uproar as the audience took sides for and against the play throughout its performance. Seated in the midst of the aroused spectators, William Butler Yeats realized that the era begun by the French symbolists had come to a close. After the deluge what remained? Yeats, looking ahead, could only exclaim: ". . . After Stéphane Mallarmé, after Paul Verlaine, after Gustave Moreau, after Puvis de Chavannes, after our own verse, after all our subtle colors and nervous rhythms, after the faint mixed tint of Conder, what more is possible? After us the Savage God."

III.

How should a modern reader approach Hartmann's symbolist dramas? What can be said to make it easier for a reader to penetrate the bristling thickets of stylistic affectations and mannerisms—which often cloak an insidious irony—and enjoy these dramas for the many aspects that link them to contemporary theatre? Possibly very little T. S. Eliot in an introduction to Djuna Barnes' *Nightwood* spoke of the impertinence of trying to talk about a work that exists almost completely within the context of its uniqueness. In fact, Ezra Pound said much the same thing about Hartmann's *Confucius,* referring to it as one of those infrequent works about which literary discussion is virtually useless. Pound found it a very difficult play to get into and yet "very beautiful after one has gotten into it."

Some readers find it easy to accept the literary histrionics of Hartmann's dramas. Other readers are irritated and put off by a writer who employs the entire arsenal of symbolist techniques and devices and a metaphorical language that frequently violates all diction and syntax. The plays are packed with bizarre and infuriating solecisms, coined words, stylistic parodies mocking their period's rhetoric, bewildering jumps between scenes that leave unexplained gaps, characters that assume significance one moment only to disappear without warning, and a casual attitude towards style that expresses itself in the author's slipping back and forth from prose to *vers libre* and rhyme whenever he feels so inclined. Is Hartmann serious? Sometimes—sometimes not!

To the generation of American artists with whom Hartmann associated at the Cafe Manhattan, Grape Vine, Cafe Francis, and Bohemian gatherings, the idea of the *premier coup* was all-important. Even making sketches was looked on with contempt: why not produce a masterpiece on the first try? Spontaneity also was critically significant to the symbolists, although such poets as Mallarmé, who refined their verse for years before deciding upon publication, understood that spontaneity was primarily an illu-

sion—the product of skillfully arranged disorder. Hartmann's approach to his dramas was much the same as the
painters who defended the *premier coup*. Nothing could go
wrong if one followed the authentic moments of inspiration.
In this respect, Hartmann anticipates Jack Kerouac's notion
of automatic writing. He is also a sort of William Burroughs
of the Mauve Decade—shuffling ideas and literary techniques like a deck of cards, convinced that something
worthwhile will turn up in the process.

The problem is that such approaches rarely produce the
cohesion of great works of art; their virtue is that something
strikingly original or new may emerge. Indeed, Hartmann's
dramas, violating all the rules of American drama in his
time, pioneer many techniques and conventions of the
modern theatre, particularly the Theatre of the Absurd and
the more recent guerilla theatre of revolt. Hartmann would
have agreed with Apollinaire that the playwright is the God
of the universe he creates and should employ all of the
"mirages at his disposal." Among Hartmann's many mirages
was the introduction of motion color (anticipating the
psychedelic light show) in the last scene of *Buddha,* despite
the fact that he recognized that no machinery yet existed to
project the effects he wanted.

Although critics argued that many of the scenic effects
called for by Hartmann in his dramas could not be produced, his familiarity with stagecraft from its early history
to the Saxe-Meiningen methods and those of the Royal
Theatres, Munich, persuaded him otherwise. He considered all of his dramas "playable, but just like Wagner's,
not for the ordinary stage." While Hartmann never found a
Debussy to orchestrate his dramas as did Maeterlinck, they
were intended for production accompanied by music,
dance, song, and such new arts as the perfume concert and
motion color, which he believed technically feasible and
hovering on the horizon of the twentieth century. Perhaps

one can best image what Hartmann had in mind for his dramas if in reading *Confucius,* for example, where the social satire still possesses a sharp edge, one conceives of a production somewhat on the order of *Marat-Sade* with musical bridges at appropriate intervals and choruses introducing the frequent delegations that beseige the Chinese philosopher. Although there is much of the spectacle to Hartmann's plays, he also intended that the scenic ornamentation be subordinate to the work and its ideas. Stagecraft for Hartmann was a skillful accessory and accompaniment to atmosphere. "What is the use of my writing a *Buddha,*" he asked, "if Gordon Craig would make a Gordon Craig out of it." He told Craig as much during their correspondence in the 1920's, even as he admitted great admiration for Craig's genius.

Just as Jarry's *Ubu Roi* was described by Sacha Guitry as a phenomenon in the realm of "excessive caricature," so Hartmann in one of his few statements about his dramas described them as "intellectual caricature in the tradition of Aubrey Beardsley." Despite their episodic construction, Hartmann insisted that his dramas possessed a subterranean unity: "In writing my dramas, I was at times conscious of a distinct feeling of some underlying line idea; a straight soaring obtuse angle for *Buddha;* a vast ellipse not meeting at the ends for *Mohammed;* a vast plane with protuberances for *Confucius;* and the ordinary pyramid or half circle conception of a dramatic plot from beginning to climax and end for *Christ.*"

Hartmann infuses his drama with much that is pure abstract theatre, employing non-literary traditions that extend from the horseplay of the *mimus* of antiquity to the type of vaudeville patter and pantomime he enjoyed in New York Bowery burlesque houses of the 1890's. A variety of disparate theatrical antecedents and symbolistic techniques are combined to produce a drama which is characterized by

such elements as allusive and imagistic language; the evoca-
tion of indefinite moods and feelings; choreographic and
vaudeville type situations; verbal punning, coining of neolo-
gisms, and the use of portmanteau words; a dehumanizing
and typifying of characters into stylized choral figures
exemplifying abstract ideas; soliloquy-type speeches;
dreamlike stage settings and scenery; and sheer spectacle—the appearance of jugglers, circus animals, and gor-
geously panoplied processions.

The tone of Hartmann's dramas is primarily one of
elusive irony. That irony is least evident in his earliest
work, *Christ*, where the poetic passages are seriously inten-
tioned even if they verge at times on Swinburnean parody.
The lushness of similar passages in *Buddha*, however, are
the work of an older Hartmann, now writing not only in the
symbolist mode but having fun satirizing it as well. In
Buddha, Hartmann piles symbolist effect on symbolist effect. He loads the drama with many of the stock icons of
symbolist verse and painting: swans, lotuses, incense, diseased bodies, and the crimson blood of the dying. He romps
around with many of the literary and philosophical schools
of his time. He particularly enjoys poking fun at certain
symbolist works and conventions. In *Buddha*, for example,
the soliloquy of the Barbarian Chieftain, delivered as he
stands on the cleft skull of his father, is a sly echo of the
monologue over Yorick's skull in Jules Laforgue's *Hamlet.* In
the punctuated silences between lines of Buddha's Nirvana
monologue, one catches a spoofing of the famed Maeter-
linckian silences.

There is little that was later attempted by the surrealists,
dadaists, expressionists, and later exponents of the Theatre
of the Absurd that cannot be glimpsed somewhere in
Hartmann's dramas and that is not encompassed in his
vision of what the theatre might become if the playwright's
imagination were given free reign. Even the gory corpses

that litter the stage in various scenes of *Buddha* and the dying famine victims gnawing the bones of the already dead in *Confucius* anticipate that eerie mass of bodies outside the window of a home in Jean Tardieu's *Qui Est Là* (1947). The dialogue between Kung and the Emperor in *Confucius,* both buried to their necks in rice, has its analogue in Samuel Beckett's *Happy Days* (1961), where the anti-heroine Winnie sinks into a mound of earth during the course of the play until only her head protrudes.

All of Hartmann's dramas are united by a single central concept: the efforts of man to impose his will upon exterior reality and shape it into an acceptable universe. Because life consists of a pageant of characters who come and go, each with conflicting aims, ideologies, and obsessions, the world is necessarily absurd. Jeshua in *Christ* is successful in opposing his will to the world and is rewarded by the appearance of a halo around his head as the curtain falls on Act III. Buddha recognizes the futility of exerting his will against the forces of reality and discovers his own reality of Nirvana. In *Buddha,* it is the characters other than the world redeemer who struggle to change exterior reality. Confucius, on the other hand, has given up the struggle of will against reality, recognizing that he is powerless to change the destiny of others and that it doesn't really matter. Yet there is an irony in the fact that each of these seers do have an impact on the world, the individuality of their wills being reflected in the converts who follow them or who will come after.

The world redeemers of Hartmann's dramas only remotely mirror the theological and ideological systems and known biographical facts about the lives of their namesakes. *Christ* does to some extent follow biblical tradition, also relying on apocryphal material from D. F. Strauss' *Life of Jesus* (1835). *Buddha* should no more be taken as a literal guide into the intricacies of Indian Buddhism, however, than should

xlii

Herman Hesse's *Siddhartha.* In *Confucius,* Hartmann scrambles Chinese history as it suits his purpose, and even deliberately drags in philosophers from other eras as foils for Kung. Believing that all religions have some virtue and that the founders of such systems are amalgams of saint and charlatan, the body of their teachings usually representing final distortions of disciples, Hartmann chose to invent freely and use his charismatic seers as vehicles for his own ideas. Although *Buddha* tends to be a little more in keeping with historical and religious reality than *Confucius,* this is purely accidental. Any literary work critical and prescriptive of reality (with a soupçon of misanthropy thrown in) is bound to sound somewhat Buddhistic simply because Buddhism was fundamentally at odds with social concerns. In contrast, *Confucius* fails as a Confucian statement for the same reason *Buddha* partially succeeds: Confucianism was wholly concerned with society and believed in its ultimate value, seeking no good outside of the social context.

Man as seen by Hartmann in his dramas is a prey to "maenad intoxication and dervish spin." He is ruled by unconcious forces (Sadakichi preferred Edueard von Hartmann's metaphysical theory of the "unconscious" to that of Freud) which are forever breaking out in holocausts of violence and massacre. A victim of his own lust, greed, hatred, and insatiable materialism, man seeks through many contorted notions of reality to escape alienation. The paths to freedom, however, may quite possibly exist only for those world redeemers who introduce new religions and thereby new confusions for those who become their disciples. Who among men except Hartmann's Jeshua in *Christ* would possess the will to scorn the carnal temptations of the seductive Queen Zenobia? "Follow me to deny your faith!" says Gautama in *Buddha* to the five Holy Disciples who have learned nothing after already following him for more than twenty years. "Abandon hope!" urges Confucius repeatedly to those delegations of zealots who visit him ever hopeful of new solutions.

HARRY LAWTON AND GEORGE KNOX

A Note on the Text and Acknowledgements

The editors have examined a number of typewritten and holograph manuscripts of *Confucius, Buddha,* and *Christ* in the Sadakichi Hartmann Archives at the University of California Library, Riverside, and in the collections of other libraries. Most of these manuscripts contain various insertions, deletions, and alterations in the texts of the dramas as originally published. Hartmann left no definitive revised texts that were marked as such. The editors have therefore taken the liberty of determining which changes are improvements that should be accepted and which should be ignored. Hartmann at one point appears to have decided to omit a scene from one of the dramas (the dance sequence in Act III of *Christ*), and after careful deliberation we decided to retain this scene. In a few cases, we have supplied missing stage directions. We have also standardized the format of all three plays.

We wish to express our gratitude to the literary executrix of the Sadakichi Hartmann estate, Mrs. Wistaria Hartmann Linton, Riverside, whose collection of her father's papers and manuscripts has again been made available for our research. Appreciation for continuing help is also due to Mrs. Dorothea Atma Gilliland of St. Petersburg, Florida, Hartmann's eldest daughter, and other members of the Hartmann family. We particularly wish to acknowledge the cooperation and assistance of libraries whose research, reference, and archive staffs have made accessible variant texts of the dramas, searched out and xeroxed other materials, and promptly responded to inquiries. Specifically, in this regard, we want to thank the University of California Library, Riverside; the Riverside Public Library; the New York Public Library; the Boston Public Library; Yale University Library; the University of Oregon Library; and the library of the Historical Society of Pennsylvania. We are greatly indebted to Dr. Marshall Van Deusen of the Department of English, University of California, Riverside, who three years ago encouraged us to embark upon Hartmann research and whose invaluable advice we have continued to seek. We are grateful to Mr. Charles Feinberg of Detroit for permitting us to examine his rare copy of Hartmann's undated symbolist broadside titled "Poems." Mr. Michael Elderman, who is carrying out bibliographical research on Hartmann, has assisted with numerous contributions. Our indebtedness for helpful readings on the plays and useful commentary is extended to several colleagues at UCR: Drs. Richard Tuerk (English), Roger N. Pierce (Drama), Francis H. Cook (Religious Studies), Henry W. Decker (French), and Ben F. Stoltzfus (French). Dr. Stoltzfus also provided an English translation of Mallarmé's letter on *Christ* that excellently renders the nuances of the French original. We also wish to express our thanks for suggestions to Patricia Beck, Victoria Hearne, and John Bosak. In addition, we appreciate the efforts of Mrs. Clara Dean, our typist, who must have encountered many difficulties in deciphering our collations and changes in format. Finally, we should like to thank the American Philosophical Society for a grant-in-aid without which publication of these dramas would have been delayed.

Confucius

A Drama in Two Acts

(Written 1894-1916; 1920-1922)

Persons Represented

KUNG, *known as "Confucius," a philosopher*
HOUSE LEEK, *his wife*
MEE NANG } *their sons*
YUEN LING }
FEE FEE, *their daughter*
KUNG'S MOTHER
FO PA, *Kung's cousin*
MUSKCOLLECTOR *and his wife*
GRASSHOPPERHUNTER and his wife
TOOTHPULLER and his wife   *relatives of*
BONECARVER and his wife   KUNG'S *wife*
COFFINPAINTER and his wife
GAMBLINGHOUSEKEEPER and his wife
JEN HWAY } *pupils of* KUNG
MANG LO }
CHWANG CHOW, *a philosopher*
LIANG KHAN, *his pupil*
A MOTHER
A CHILD
BROTHER OF UGLINESS
SPOKESMAN OF THE HAVE NOTHINGS
SPOKESMAN OF THE BROTHERS OF MUTUAL PROTECTION
SPOKESMAN OF THE FREE MEN
SPOKESWOMAN OF THE LADIES' COMMITTEE OF THE ORDER
OF PURITY
FUNERAL DIRECTOR
MIDWIFE
RIVER POLICEMAN

3

FIRST DOCTOR
SECOND DOCTOR
THIRD DOCTOR
FOURTH DOCTOR
FIFTH DOCTOR
SIXTH DOCTOR
FIRST MANDARIN
SECOND MANDARIN
THE EMPEROR
THE EMPRESS
THE DOWAGER EMPRESS
MASTER OF CEREMONIES
FIRST SECRETARY
SECOND SECRETARY
THIRD SECRETARY
FIRST ARTIST-ARTISAN
SECOND ARTIST-ARTISAN
FIRST PAINTER
SECOND PAINTER
FIRST ARCHITECT
SECOND ARCHITECT
FIREWORKER
FIRST LANDSCAPE GARDENER
SECOND LANDSCAPE GARDENER
THIRD LANDSCAPE GARDENER
COOK, *with attendants*
RICH MERCHANT
JAILER
KANG, *a crook*
THE PRINCE OF THIEVES
CHILD MURDERER

Inhabitants of the Floating Street, Retinue of Mandarins, Soldiers; Delegations of the Have Nothings, Brothers of Mutual Protection, Free Men and Ladies' Committee of the Order of Purity, Retinue of Emperor, Palanquin Bearers, The Bloody Marquise, Prisoners, Starved Villagers.

Synopsis

ACT I

On the Yellow River

PRELUDE: *The stage presents the gambol of Wind and Sun-light, amidst heavy clouds of fog and sluggish waves. Slowly a Sampan with bulging sails works its way out of the wall of mist, becomes plainly visible and, showered for a moment with sun rays, fades away in the everchanging vapor formations of the river. Thereupon the mist dispels and reveals the following.*

SCENE: *A floating Village of houseboats and bamboo floats with rice fields. In the middle foreground Kung's Houseboat of open bamboo work with picturesque mat sails. Its hull is divided into a sectional view of the three decks connected by stairs. On the upper deck,* KUNG'S PUPILS *debate; on the middle deck,* KUNG'S WIFE *lies dying; on the lower deck,* KUNG'S MOTHER *awaits a delivery. To this Houseboat a number of others are attached, connected with each other by bridges. One of them is fitted up like a temple; another like a pawnshop; a third like a restaurant with green shutters and red paper streamers.*

During the whole act, the VILLAGERS *move about this floating street according to their occupation and incidents of the play.*

In the far distance, Scenery of the embankment and glimpses of the animated traffic of the river population.

KUNG, *at the stern on the upper deck, in a soiled, patched shiftlike garment, hauling in a huge kite in the shape of a dragon,* MANG LO *and* JEN HWAY *converse. A black sow, Confucius' pet, lies at the entrance of the staircase.*

6

MANG LO. So you intend to write your philosophical conversations with Confucius. I do not like the idea. It is as difficult to appreciate the greatness of a man previous to his death as afterwards.

JEN HWAY. What you say is true enough, Mang Lo, but the number of admirers increases. They need some guidance. Now nobody notices this houseboat. In centuries hence, they will have it in some museum, and guides will point out to throngs of visitors: This is the deck where he paced to and fro developing his ideas, that is the place where Confucius generally conversed with his pupils, this is the couch whereupon he slept. And the crowd will murmur in low tones of curiosity. Now and then somebody will exclaim: "What a great man!" and a sentimental lady will sigh and roll her eyes.

MANG LO. Such admiration, as you know, is merely habitual, Jen Hway. I am convinced that he will never be admired more than by us two. His teachings will steadily grow in popularity, for that very reason, become more like dead prototypes than really influential guides of life. To the badgers with what a man is on earth, after his death.

JEN HWAY. I think at times that he is too condensed, Mang Lo. To wade through his wisdom will become a bore. I pity the students of the competitive examinations, who up to the age of fourscore years will have to comment in solitary cells on his theories, for there is no doubt to my mind that his books will become Classics.

KUNG. No chance for aerial navigation in this crawling breeze! [*Puts aside kite and steps up to pupils.*] Today we will get in only a few words edgeways. All sorts of things may happen. [*Scratches his head.*] What were you jabbering about, fame? [*Takes a paper from his sleeves.*] Look here, a lyric on dim mirrors and last year's fans, a good one, I am its author. Nobody has read it. Nobody will, most likely. [*Throws paper into river, despite protestations of his pupils.*] The wind may

7

take it to some friend of rhyme; no, it is falling in spirals like an autumn leaf—there it floats—perchance some one will rescue it; more likely, soaked with water, it will sink to the bottom of oblivion. Such are the chances for fame.

MANG LO. No matter, Master, whether a thought is published or destroyed, the result remains the same.

JEN HWAY. Could the best known poem—yours on withered hollyhocks, for example—reveal more greatness than you just have shown.

KUNG. Who can tell! What man calls greatness is merely the ability of selecting and developing the part which is great originally. [*Busies himself with regilding an old idol.*] How many things need regilding in this world.

MANG LO. If people could only understand you, Master.

JEN HWAY. That one should be so wise and the rest so stupid.

KUNG. I do not care to have them understand me. How can a man be satisfied with another's ideas unless he has none himself?

JEN HWAY. Are not some men's ideas so taut that nobody can skip over them!

KUNG. It is difficult to conceal a snoring man. Yet we are all under mutual obligations to each other, a little more or less, what is the difference!

MANG LO. But does not philosophy bring about reformations of the general condition of things?

KUNG. Who can tell! And what is there to be admired about it? Everything is well enough as it is. Changes rarely do any good. To accomplish a reformation demands many sacrifices and is generally not worthy of them. Recall the Manchurian Revolution. New ideas refuse to become common property, until so-called modern sages flabbergast the world with others. Abandon hope, my boy.

JEN HWAY [sighs]. Quite so, what can we expect! Look at those men and women, Mang Lo, how they lounge there in the afternoon heat, all hungry with desire, the fulfillment of which would break conventional laws. They do not dare to do anything and censure those who make the attempt. So they waste their lives, drinking, wenching, gambling, talking all day long and when evening has come not even remembering what they have said.

KUNG. That is their affair. One cannot prescribe happiness.

JEN HWAY. Do you not teach, Master, that every being should live to develop its individuality?

KUNG. So they do, in their way; to what purpose, who can tell.

[*A* CHILD, *all wet, comes climbing up to the deck.*]

CHILD'S MOTHER. What, did you climb on the outside of the boat again? Did I not tell you not to do it. You have spoilt your dress.

CHILD. I was trying to dip the sun out of the water. I was sure I would get hold of him, but he always slipped away.

CHILD'S MOTHER. Nonsense! [*Cuffs* CHILD'S *ears.*]

JEN HWAY. Why not let the child express its desires! Why wait until other less beautiful thoughts perturb its mind? He will remember your unkindness.

CHILD'S MOTHER. Oh, children so easily forget.

MANG LO. So you think children do not suffer, aye? Rest assured they have their cares and sorrows, despairs and tragic sufferings like grown persons, different, of course, but equally intense. And the parents are the cause of their sufferings. They rule them according to impulses, agreeable or disagreeable, just as the hour may bring them. Husband and wife have quarreled and the child gets licked for it. The parents should remember that the family represents the entire life to a child.

CHILD. Because Ma is big she thinks she can torment me. I never know what those head-in-the-airs are up to. I know only by my backside whether I did right or wrong.

9

KUNG. Now, there you see.

CHILD'S MOTHER. Oh, children are so full of moods.

MANG LO. Their necessary wants seem moods to you. Children are not yet well-regulated automatons in which every wheel turns at a certain moment to accomplish a certain movement. Too early the melodies of life are drowned in the monotonous rhythms of social laws.

CHILD'S MOTHER. Do I not spend all my time in teaching him how to behave, how to bow and lift his feet and not to sneeze in company? [KUNG *laughs*.]

JEN HWAY. Woman, there is nothing natural in a sway or dip.

MANG LO You think it sufficient to feed and cloth a child, to protect it from dangers and to love it blindly. The supreme duty of fatherhood and motherhood, good woman, is to comprehend your children. Realize that they have a soul, thoughts and emotions of their own, try to penetrate into their inner nature and see things as they see them.

CHILD'S MOTHER [*to* KUNG]. Is that the fruit of your teaching? Men who have theories never live up to them. I know so much.

KUNG. We all ride in creaking carriages. There is no particular use in lecturing and advising people. They do not want to know any better. Nevertheless, children suffer largely for the shortcomings of grown up folks. And you [*kicks child with his foot*] have only one remedy—your lack of reasoning power.

CHILD. Mother, a kash for a vegetable pie.

CHILD'S MOTHER. Don't bother me, ask those men who talk so wisely.

CHILD. Then I'll swipe one.

CHILD'S MOTHER. You good for nothing monkey! [*Gives him a beating; while doing so, child steals a kash from her sleeve.*]

10

MANG LO [*laughs*].   You have the talent for a clever thief.

CHILD'S MOTHER [*out of breath*].   Now, surely that ain't right.

KUNG [*shrugs his shoulders*].   Who can tell! In case he should have special gifts for stealing, he may be truly happy only while practicing them and thus be of more use to the final evolution of things by being perfect in that exciting—to others rather unpleasant—occupation than by remaining an ordinary average being without impulses of any sort.

CHILD'S MOTHER.   It is criminal to talk that way. I would drown him this very moment if I knew. [*Exit grumbling.*]

MANG LO.   Better tell him "A Dream of the Red Chamber."

JEN HWAY.   Master, won't you quote the passage in parental duties to us.

KUNG [*yawning*].   Can't you think of anything else to bother me! How often do you want me to repeat it? Of course, I know—see that you get it down right this time. [*Jen Hway takes notes.*] "Parents, love your children however ungrateful they may prove to be, however much they may go astray, always remember that you are the sole cause of their existence, and that all kindnesses lavished upon them will never outweigh the agony of their existence. If they do not want to work, go to work for them. You have no right to ask anything of them. Teach them to be men and women; if they turn out failures or crippled nonentities, pity them and repay their evil doings with renewed love, for through you they are what they are." They are entitled to a seat in your ox-cart.

JEN HWAY [*eagerly*].   And the children?

KUNG.   Insatiable one! Should be willing—provided the parents have done their duty—to give up every pleasure and treasure, accept any dishonor, perpetrate any crime for them out of their own free will, because through their

11

parents they are what they are. But enough of this. [*Descends the staircase to the middle deck.* JEN HWAY *and the black sow follow him.*]

[FEE FEE *sits on the staircase.*]

KUNG. Humming songs all day.

FEE FEE. Have I been singing—I thought—[*Looks at two butterflies gamboling in the hatchway.*]

HOUSE LEEK [*lying on a couch*]. Where did you stay so long, Fucie! Why do you not come to me? You know I may die at any moment, perhaps this afternoon.

KUNG. You have jabbered in that strain for months. [*Goes to staircase of lower deck.*] Has the midwife arrived?

KUNG'S MOTHER [*seated in bed, wearing enormous spectacles with broad rims of tortoise shell, she groans at short intervals*]. Oh, there is plenty of time.

KUNG. Pretty close, I would say, as you have pains at such short intervals.

KUNG'S MOTHER. Did you ever give birth to a child? Surely, I should know.

JEN HWAY. How many will it make?

KUNG. Twenty-four; isn't that right, Mother? [*Puts screen before Mother's couch.*]

KUNG'S MOTHER. Twenty-four, what an idea! It's the twenty-fifth, you sconce. Only one more and I will win the great Peking prize. I never had any use for robes, I wore a wrapper all my life.

JEN HWAY. The blessings of the gods, must rest upon your house. My venerable mother brought it only to sixteen.

KUNG [*on staircase between middle and upper deck*]. A goodly number after all, if you take into consideration that the worthy lady of my temporary domiciles produced only one set of twins during twenty years of matrimonial agonies.

HOUSE LEEK. How mean always to mention that.

KUNG. It is a fact, is it not! I am not complaining.

HOUSE LEEK. But I do not care to hear it mentioned all

12

the time. It is not right to talk of your dying wife in such a way.

KUNG. Now, can you not keep quiet! What is the use of unnecessarily exciting yourself?

HOUSE LEEK. You give me good cause, you lazy man, talking that way in my death hour, after all I have suffered with you, oh my! Oh, my!

KUNG [*returning with* JEN HWAY *to the upper deck.*]. Infants are like kittens. You can train them to obedience and cleanliness. We managed to leave ours alone for hours. They were put into a tea chest, and told to go asleep. [*Chuckles, busies himself with boiling some rice.*]

JEN HWAY. I shall have as few children as possible. I consider that a poor man's duty.

MANG LO. You think too much about it, you ought to be a conception evader.

MANG LO. The white forces of life dribble away only in two ways, either [*points to his forehead*] or [*points to his lower body*]. Although we should not have more children than we can bring up decently, it is better to have too many than none. A way to take care of them can always be found. It doubles, trebles a man's activity.

JEN HWAY. And makes a slave of the woman and ruins her health.

KUNG. Not if she be normal. No, let Chinese women always remain hot, violent mothers. In order that they may, let us remain conservative, adverse to foreign influences. Culture aspiring too much towards the ideal, bears the germ of decay within itself. Men become less natural, women less healthy. The pure in sex will steadily decrease. Females will have fewer children and the nation be less powerful. Let us remain as we are. The other nations will mount by apparent self-improvement to self-ruin. We are so mighty in stability that even if we were conquered, our vast majority would assimilate our barbarian conquerors.

13

YUEN LING [*enters with* BROTHER OF UGLINESS]. Father, a Brother of Ugliness wants to pay his respects to you. I wish I were one of them. If you don't mind, father, I'll give it a trial and go with him.

KUNG [*shrugs his shoulders, to the* BROTHER OF UGLINESS]. Salutations!

JEN HWAY. I suppose, Brother, you worship ugliness as some men love an ugly wench with a secret pride in loving something rare and exclusive, the enjoyment of which nobody is particularly anxious to share.

BROTHER OF UGLINESS. Ung, ung! young sage, evil spirits must have invented beauty for torment and distress. Oh, soft, intimate, life-rejuvenating ideal of ugliness! For us the world moves on in undisturbed harmonies. We know no unaccomplished desire. The natural development of human conditions calmly and steadily proceeds. We do not hope that an ideal unreached today will be ours tomorrow. The demands of beauty are brutal insolence. Our ideals are shaped in such a way that reality has room in them. [KUNG'S MOTHER *groans below.*] The entire world belongs to us. We enjoy it like a dream of animated pictures in which the ideal often seems inferior to reality.

KUNG. As in all assertions, there is some truth in yours. Verily, verily. I say unto you, hope is as great an error as hypocrisy. How can we enjoy life, constantly expecting something better to turn up.

BROTHER OF UGLINESS. Ung, ung! That is the reason why life to most of you is so stale and dark, so narrow and contorted. The ideal of beauty looms radiant and spotless before you. It knows no pity and condemns all that is not perfect, destroying the calm enjoyments of half satisfied desires. We take the world as it is. Our senses are rich and deep enough for that.

YUEN LING. And would I find satisfaction there! Life is

14

so short we should choose the right path. It seems most people don't, so many are misplaced.

BROTHER OF UGLINESS. Silence you will find in our mountain monasteries. We are well versed in the art of solitude. Whether you will find peace depends on you alone. It will take years before you reach that haven of rest. Twenty long years you will have to devote to the worship of Ugliness. The petty cares of life will not bother you. You will receive enough to subsist, no more. [KUNG *grins*.] Life will flow on smoothly. You will be in the very midst of it, yet feel as if you were apart. Our lips are not burnt dry from incessant prayer like flower beds frowsed and dust-storm-swept. You may be sent to the famine district, to bitter sands where white bones fall to ashes in the heat, where in crumbling huts, remnants of human beings, too feeble to sit or stand, stare into the dark blue desert until death comes to gather them in.

KUNG. You will make a sort of charity tramp of him.

BROTHER OF UGLINESS. Or you may be ordered to some infant refuge, thronged with little transients from all nooks and corners of human misery, where night upon night death stalks, lifting little souls from the couches into his bony arms. And in their places come others with pain distorted faces, pale clammy hands, and large enquiring eyes. The cots are never empty, nor the coffins. May Ugliness enlighten you! Ung, Ung! [*Exit with* YUEN LING.]

KUNG [*contemplates the formation of craters and their eruptions on the surface of the boiling rice*].

CHWANG CHOW [*enters with* LIANG KHAN]. You are Confucius. I recognize you by your fat round nose and the exposure of your front teeth. My name is Chwang Chow, poet-philosopher, disciple of Lao-tse.

KUNG. Can I offer you a dish of rice?

LIANG KHAN. We came to talk with you.

15

KUNG. Did you not read my books? They really contain all I have to say.

CHWANG CHOW. Yes, we read your Book of Changes, your History, your Book of Rites, and your State Religion. I would be pleased to discuss some points with you.

KUNG. You know, you have views different to mine. Of what use is arguing?

CHWANG CHOW. To sharpen our convictions.

KUNG. Mine are sharp enough.

LIANG KHAN [aside]. Disagreeably haughty. [Half aloud to CHWANG CHOW.] Come, let us go. His realm lies here. He is not interested in that. [Pointing to the sky where a reddish sun is struggling through grey clouds.]

KUNG. I gave such things their due. The red tints of maple leaves, the belling of deer in autumn and all that! I made a Collection of National Poetry.

CHWANG CHOW. Then you acknowledge that not everything must be of immediate use, that something can exist simply for its own intrinsic value, without any definable purpose.

KUNG. Do not most things exist that way?

CHWANG CHOW. Why not speculative philosophy?

KUNG. No objection. It does exist, does it not?

CHWANG CHOW. The poets write for the poets, the painters paint for the painters, why should not philosophers—

KUNG. A philosopher should suggest—not teach—practical ways to make life more tolerable—not better, mind you.

CHWANG CHOW. Is even that possible? There are a few people who live hundreds of years ahead of their time, and others who lag hundreds of years behind. Yet most people live in all times, and as we cannot fathom the various conditions of human minds, of what use is teaching but for the few! How can we in our darkness enlighten others. Did

16

you not argue somewhat like that yourself in your Book on—

KUNG. No matter what book. As we are influenced by invisible substances and forces, unknown to us, we can comprehend only the actual and that badly enough. We are like a flock of sheep scurrying over the plain of thought, goaded from one to another more wretched pasture. You do not care for any rice, well, pardon me if I help myself to some. Yet you want to explain realms beyond truth? What for! I know the mob. They have never learnt to be frank about others, how much less about themselves. Why should they know Truth, or even something beyond it! Stretch your arm to things that are within reach. Let out all the powers you possess in some no matter what channel. To have an aim in life is life and nothing further.

CHWANG CHOW. It takes a philosopher to appreciate those sentences.

KUNG. Who can tell! But if I advise a people "Not to cook dumplings in a teapot" or that "Also the Yellow River"—you would probably say The Golden River from the Sea of Stars—is sometimes clear—they understand me. As for the rest, I do not know, and do not care to come to any final conclusion as men cannot know.

CHWANG CHOW. And the hereafter?

KUNG. I am sure I know less than you about it. I hope they have enough rice to eat over there. But now kindly favor somebody else with your presence. I have to take care of my illustrious grandchild for a while.

MEE NANG [*ushers in the Delegation of* HAVE NOTHINGS]. A delegation of the Have Nothings, venerable father.

KUNG. Botheration! You see they keep me busy. Let me not detain you from going along your flowery starlit road, Chwang Chow. I'll try to crawl over my one pole bridge to some place where I may sit down quietly and take a nap. If there is a bridge from the beginning to the end, it is finer than hair and sharper than the edge of a sword. [*Sits down*

17

with baby in one arm, leaning the other elbow on the flanks of his black sow. CHWANG CHOW *and* LIANG KHAN *exit.*]

SPOKESMAN OF THE HAVE NOTHINGS.   We are the Have Nothings. We do all the hard work. We work on the highways, carry stones, dig, fell and cleave trees, and just get so much that we have nothing. We come to you for advice. We can never earn more than we absolutely need; if we are out of work we have to starve. And even when we work we are in need of the actual necessities of life. We are crushed by overwork, notwithstanding we have nothing. Want of nourishment, want of clothing, want of housing, want of everything that renders life in ever so little a degree agreeable. Our children cannot satisfy their hunger. They go to spelling contests with empty stomachs. We must have rice for those famished little beings before education becomes profitable. Nobody would dare to dispute these facts.

KUNG.   True, but what are we going to do about it?

MANG LO.   Can you men do anything else but hand and back labor? Can you draw the plan for a bridge? Must not always somebody produce by other efforts than calloused palms the opportunities for the hod-carrying you do?

HAVE NOTHINGS.   We did not come to talk to a boy. We want the government to own all land and property, all tools and means of production, all the booths of traffic. The government shall be everything and supervise everything. All persons—the master who sits in his pavilion and the servant who sits in the outhouse—should have equal opportunities of education, so that all dormant faculties may have a chance to be developed. I myself might have been a philosopher, alas, the avenues of knowledge were never opened to me!

KUNG'S MOTHER [*groans below*].   I wish those men would stop their talking!

KUNG.   Would that help! Would not those who know the most take advantage of the others knowing less?

MEE NANG. Of course, father—Do you not know that the little you can ever own, must be, wrung by sheer force from that monster which you trust so blindly. Do you not know—you ought to—that it is the government which faithfully aids the rich in reducing the workingman by weapons of law, of hunger and force into actual bondage? Only with a stinkpot in your hand or a two-blade sword in your fists can you tear from the vampire a portion of that which might have come to you from the progress of centuries. No, my friends, every grain of silver earned, every freedom gained in your workshop, will be marked by corpses—yours and those of your kin.

HAVE NOTHINGS. We do not care what you say. You are a revoltist. We want no rebellion. Our wives and children suffer enough without it. We want to hear the man from the Yellow River talk.

KUNG. I wish you would leave me in peace. How often must I tell you, stop this everlasting belly-talk. Are we not all starving in one way or another. Abandon hope, my friends. Take life as it is. You cannot change it, for, if you could, you would. If I were obsessed to explore the cold sea of the South, if nothing else could make my life worth living, I would start off at once, even to perish in the effort. Therefore make the best of current discrepancies, my friends.

HAVE NOTHINGS. Is that all he has to say. I declare that wasn't worth coming for. He is another of those wise guys who sit and study all the time, and get no free air.

KUNG. The air is free enough here on the Yellow River.

HAVE NOTHINGS. He never gained his livelihood by the sweat of his brow—Nobody should be allowed to be a philosopher without cultivating the soil. A man who doesn't work can't have first rate health. With a second rate body he can't produce any first rate thought. He is not the man to reform society. He could never rejuvenate the world.

KUNG. My dear folks—

HAVE NOTHINGS. We want none of your sympathy. We want the government to take care of us. [*Exit growling.*]

KUNG. Well, there you have it. What is the use of worrying about anything.

FEE FEE [*passing her mother's couch*]. Mother, how can there be so much beauty in this world. I feel as if all the light centered upon me, and yet they say there is no happiness for woman in this life.

HOUSE LEEK. May the light linger upon your sweet face. Your voice, Whittle-Heart, comes to me as from afar, so strange and new, as if fairy tales of which I had not thought for a long, long time suddenly rushed back to me. [*To* KUNG, *approaching her couch.*] Are they gone at last? How I pity those poor folks!

KUNG. They are not worse off than we are.

HOUSE LEEK. You are so indifferent to everybody. No wonder they won't help you.

KUNG. I only tolerate people as I tolerate the mud on my shoes on rainy days, and yet there has been many an hour when also I gnashed my teeth, and cried out aloud in pain over all the suffering and degradation men heap upon each other and themselves. When you see me stoically sitting up there staring at the Yellow River, you do not know what currents of pain convulse my inner self. I suffer with humanity at large.

HOUSE LEEK. Oh, that old story again. I wished you showed me at least a little more sympathy. Why do you not get my coffin from the pawnshop? You know that I may die at any moment.

KUNG. That means I have to pawn the sow. I'll go, but listen to this lyric first.

HOUSE LEEK. Some other time. I am too tired. Of what use is it to write all that stuff. You cannot get it published in this country. They might arrest you again. I do not want to go through another affair like that.

KUNG. It was you who made me publish my "Sweetheart of Tethagata."

HOUSE LEEK. I thought you would gain something by it.

KUNG. And did I not? Of course nothing for the stew-pan. I suppose that is all you care for. If you had only learnt to make the best of everything, House Leek.

HOUSE LEEK. Why did you ever bring me here? Ah, how I long for the moonlit nights in my native valley where the winds combed the ghostlike hair of the willows by the stream and shook down the catkins on the winding silver of the water.

KUNG. All I ever longed for was a frail bamboo hut in some forest shade, near a pale grey lake, where convent bells toll in the distance, and there write what I want to write. [*Changes infant's underthings.*] And I did not even get that.

HOUSE LEEK. It would be a fine reward for all I have gone through with you.

KUNG. Oh, shut up!

HOUSE LEEK. Wasting away my life, my health and youth, in this miserable house boat.

KUNG. Oh, I wish I had traded you off to someone else. Why did you stay!

HOUSE LEEK. I wish you had. Even today, I would go at once, you lazy snake, you selfish toad. But nobody wants a woman having grown stale with you.

KUNG. Shut up! [*Throws a rag at her.*]

HOUSE LEEK. Oh my, oh my! I tell you, I won't forget this.

KUNG [*walks away*]. What is the use of having a virtue. If you really possess one, you bear it so naturally that nobody appreciates it, or even acknowledges that you possess it. [*Goes to the upper deck and begins to wash.*]

[MANG LO *plays on the reed flute.* FO PA *enters, with belly bulging out of his garment, big round head, braided mustache, powdered and made up with consummate art, looking juvenile despite being fifty.*]

21

KUNG [*rubbing hard*]. How fare you, cousin? The dimensions of your belly become more and more preposterous. You ought to march in the parade of pregnant women.

FO PA. Tolerable, cousin, tolerable. I manage to amuse myself. Look at my fellow students, merchants most of them, how wrinkled and worn out they look while I am as gay and juvenile as ever.

KUNG [*sniffs*]. Still odorous of grease paint. I suppose, obscene old boy, you still pursue with hot flushed cheeks, sunny youths gazing with strange and secret smiles at forest pools.

FO PA. A pretty sentence that, Confucius. I object though to the word obscene—there is nothing obscene in the world.

KUNG. Who can tell! No doubt you are right as far as you yourself are concerned. Do you still lecture on graceful deportment and read Fo-Hi and the poets?

FO PA. And you, are you still content to wallow in poverty!

KUNG. By the sun and the moon and the stars, their offspring, how dirty these rags are. He must have eaten something which did not agree with him. I am satisfied with a few kash a day.

FO PA. I want millions. I do not believe that artists should hibernate in poverty. They should revel in luxury. Every wish of theirs should be sacred. And times are changing. Artists begin to make money.

KUNG. By lowering art into trade!

FO PA. They will soon be able to rival wealth. If they would only combine to give an independent position in society, instead of catering to the rich and feeling flattered when they can dine with one of them. And instead of Prince So-And-So thinking he confers a great honor upon Kung by inviting him, he should be glad when Kung condescends to ask him to tea. Some day people may see you walking the street with a magnificent cap of satin and furs, and they will

ask who is he thus honored! It is the famous philosopher
Kung, that clever son of a god, wearing the cap that the rich
merchants of Peking presented to him. One partisan of
wealth should compete with the other in engaging poets,
artists and philosophers for their retinue. One partisan of
wealth in Nanking will say, "Kung, I will pay you twenty-
five thousand if you become my private philosopher; say
and write whatever you like, only now and then honor me at
dinner with your illustrious presence and learned conversation." Then another partisan of wealth in Tartary hearing of
this will send a most respectful petition: "What, he offers
you only twenty-five thousands—incredible! Cheap skate! I
will give you fifty thousands and not even ask you to share
my humble meals with me."

KUNG. Only the overrich can patronize art. And one
man here and there cannot be just to all tastes. The
parvenues who hoard their money by hard work and various
methods will not spend it "on seaweed drifting to the
shore" or "the leaping of trout in a mountain stream" much
less so their children who do not even own integrity. The
children of the fourth generation may appreciate "the
young shoots of the fern in spring" but they will gather
them themselves. And should ever social equality prevail
art will be dead, for nobody will have enough to afford these
luxuries of the soul.

FO PA. That's right, be an aristocrat. Now I will pay my
compliments to the excellent and venerable lady of the
house. [*Turns.*] By all the minor posts, what now!

KUNG [*studying the soap bubbles*]. Look how the colors of
the bubbles change to every changing sound of Mang Lo's
flute. [FO PA *smilingly shakes his head as he descends to the
middle deck.*]

MIDWIFE [*rushes in*]. Here I am early enough I hope!
Look at my little hand. I lift the children right out in this
way.

[KUNG *shows midwife the way to his* MOTHER, *is stopped by a*

23

Delegation of the SECRET BROTHERS, *returns to his work and hangs up the daily wash.*]

SECRET BROTHERS. We are the Secret Brothers of Success and Mutual Protection. We would like to initiate you as a member. We have formed a fraternity, the members of which are obliged to protect and aid each other. We wear crowns and white horse hair badges, hold feasts with all sorts of curious rites, midnight sorbitions, inhibitions and amatory exploitations. We have a certain way of poking each other, in this manner, to find out whether we are Secret Brothers or not. If we are, we do everything for each other, extend credit and similar privileges, as long as we do not harm ourselves, for we must be independent ourselves first to help others, you understand.

[KUNG *scratches his pate and continues to hang up wet clothes. During the following scene the* SECRET BROTHERS *leave, and* KUNG, *accompanied by his black sow, is seen sauntering to the pawnshop.*]

HOUSE LEEK [*talking to* FO PA]. Why should any mortal suffer as I have suffered! Every misfortune has been mine since the day I bound my ankle to his with the red matrimonial cords. You know what a temper he has. At first all the dreadful vicissitudes were tempered by a fanatic worship I had for the silken tassel on his hat, and even his brutal indifference did not lessen my liking for him. Like a dog I seemed to become more and more attached to my master with every kick. I know you have always sympathized with me, cousin, let me tell you some of the incidents of my mournful career.

That shabby wedding without cards and paper dragons, just as a matter of course as if nothing had happened, and imagine, he sat down on a part of my dress and never offered me a chance to sit on his, it was so short. Then the everlasting wandering from place to place, pawning every blessed article I possessed, even the flannel cushions my venerable mother gave me, and leaving naught but rags behind. I who had entertained the hope of cultivating small feet! Our wretched journey to my parents' rice farm, looking like beggars, without a kash in our sleeves, his strange haughty behavior, no wonder my venerable father treated me harshly and was glad to show me the outside of the gate two weeks before the expected birth. The arrival at Peking penniless, and my delivery of twins in a mud hovel. The incarceration for his mono-drama, an effusion which has caused me much misfortune. Weeks of running about quarreling with irate insolent innkeepers, our escapes at night from shanties where we starved, unable to pay, and we were always unable.

Then our wretched voyage to the wilds of Tartary, not as decent people travel, but in an ox-cart, and the ox was so old and ill fed, and a religious ox in the bargain, that he would stand still every few moments or from sheer habit, walk about in a circle. Oh, how I perspired under the torrid dismal desert sun. And so it went on years in years out. Nothing but chopped pork, noodles and bean cheese for steady fare. Only once at a lantern festival did we indulge in buffalo steak and roasted eggs well seasoned with age. In Tibet, where he thought he might do something, the gods alone know what, it was the same penury, tea without butter, the pawning of everything to the last breechcloth, so that I had to receive old friends of my venerable father, naked under a bamboo mat. I could not even wear one of Kung's pants, as he had only one, that one had no seat. One of the visitors, an ex-general, a lean and long-bearded imp, after allowing him, old lust-bag, to dally with my breasts, a mat does not give you much protection, procured me cotton garments and sent us by caravan to the Yellow River. Think of two months cooking and minding twins on a camel's back, more vomitive than a wretched sampan, and those changes of temperature. Here on the houseboat again starvation,

25

overwork, filth, sickness, daily lack of coin, the everlasting crying of babies, dozens of them, the annual flood, the fearful summer nights on the river with the smell of decaying things, attacks of lightning pains under the breasts and in the belly, fights with my spouse, brutally gibed at in vulgar names, everlastingly hammered at and scolded, all this tormented me to the dark verge of frenzy.

And worst of all, the constant drudgery, the never ending effort of managing to live on air and promises, to bring up offsprings halfway clean, to keep garments crisp and whole, and to get rid of daily truck accumulations. Oh drudgery kills every bud, sky blue or pink, it drains and withers, it drives to despair, all good resolves are bitten and scorched. Is it not like a grey nightmare, Cousin. Why, you have fallen asleep, Cousin. How dare you snore when I relate the real story of my life.

FO PA [*wakes up reciting*]. "And still the great river rolls its waves to the East." Oh, ahem, ha ha! I apologize, but I am a person who needs rest. I understand your situation. I have often racked my brain about it. I know all about such things. My nodding, therefore, meant no offence. I have an intellect that demands much care and attention. It is still exhausted from recent recitations. "And still—"

[KUNG *comes pulling along a coffin on the upper deck*.]

MEE NANG [*ushers in a delegation of the* FREE MEN]. Venerable father, lend an ear to the Free Men. I have joined their forces.

KUNG. Tosh!

FREE MAN. Master, we have come to you to help us to abolish government and set all men free.

KUNG. My dream for years. The speaker seems to be a miner. Those black specks ingrained into your flesh tell the story. A hard life, and nothing but the privilege to wrap yourself proudly in the raiments of poverty as recompense.

FREE MAN. No man has the right to govern men! Each

26

individual has sovereign rights by nature which are indisputably his own. Man, without his consent, should not be governed. All governments of the present day rest upon force, either of battle-axe or pike, or a bulldozed majority. All governments therefore are vicious and immoral, and the parent of all ills human society is heir to. Mankind has outgrown the need of government. Help us, illustrious sage, that the government does nothing, owns nothing, and is nothing.

FREE MEN [*shout*].   Down with governments!

KUNG.   And when every individual is free to make its own regulations of conduct, will the latter not be as inconvenient to some as much as ever. It cannot be otherwise. Human beings, each and all, are too mean and narrow for the upward climb.

FREE MAN.   Only experience and knowledge will be relied upon to the practical ideals of civilization, master. The rights of all will be secure, because the rights of every being will be recognized.

KUNG.   Of every one in particular! How and by whom! [*Shakes his head.*] Only few are firm-legged enough to stand on their own authority.

FREE MAN.   Down with authority! Down with morality, law, religion!

KUNG.   A cook is needed even for the most frugal brew.

MEE NANG.   Father, do you not understand, they want that everybody governs himself.

KUNG.   Yes, to be sure, for that we need no future era. That is what everybody could do now. Are you so thick-pated as to believe that sandstorms and floods will cease!

FREE MAN.   Then you do not endorse our hopes!

KUNG.   Abandon hope, my friends. Things will ever be as they are now. Somebody will always be obliged to make concessions. Conditions may grow a little better or worse. What of that! You reason tolerably well, but pardon me if I cannot greet you as heroes of emancipation, the deliverers from mundane woes.

FREE MAN. Surely, you do not object—?

KUNG. Object! Why should I object? Prune away as much as you like, and enjoy the fruits if there are any. I know you want to allow everything to everybody, and for that reason, deem it wise to talk for years, and now and then throw a stinkpot into the houses of harmless villagers, or to stab a prince. Now if the throwing of stinkpots pleases you, go on. If you can possibly manage do not throw them right into my houseboat here; if you must do so, I suppose I will have to make the best of it, as I am somewhat a thrower of stinkpots myself, only of a different brand.

MEE NANG. Father, father, do you not see as plainly as waves breaking on the beach, that all the wrongs and abuses of our present day community spring directly or indirectly from government. Down with the government that debases men, traffics women, corrupts our children, trammels love, stifles thought, monopolizes land, robs labor of its rewards, and fosters the vile privileges of wealth and power.

KUNG. Join them, if your heart prompts you, my boy, yet consider—whether it is worth while that we two lose each other for the sake of a stinkpot—for I know you will throw yours into places they never dared to dream about.

MEE NANG. Father, I cannot help it. Revolt alone will save the poor from utter bondage. [*The disgusted* FREE MEN *leave noisily.*]

KUNG. I sometimes wonder that not all in this wide world of drudgery turn to revolt. Day by day, from morn to night, each man must go his dreary way to the end! To eat and clothe himself and be sheltered against heat or cold. How much better to be one of the wandering tribes of Tartary. He hunts, eats what nature offers, clothes himself in the skins of wild animals and sleeps under the open sky. Happiness indeed! Alas, we would miss the so-called city life. To be huddled together, to array ourselves according to the latest dictates of fashion, to peruse the Imperial Gazette, to toil for food and shelter and vegetate in sober domesticity. The strong breeze of the steppes has become too strong for us. That would be an approach to ideal life. Notwithstanding I sit in this houseboat here and ruminate—instead of galloping on a vigorous steed over the plains of Tartary.

[*The* SIX DOCTORS *enter with medicine boxes, incense, swords and brooms.*]

FIRST DOCTOR.   We have come for a final consultation.

KUNG.   To kill her, I fancy. Well, what do you intend to do?

THE SIX DOCTORS.   First, we must bow three times to the right, then to the left and slide about in a circle. [*They act as they say.*] Thereupon we burn these yellow papers. [*Produce some yellow paper strips with printed hieroglyphics and light them.*] Sweep the ground of all impurities, and chase the evil spirits! [*Sweep and cut the air with their swords.*]

KUNG.   A venerable occupation that.

FIRST DOCTOR.   Kung, I am sure if you had put your wife—at the right moment entirely in my care, I would have cured her. Even now, not too late. You see, certain points rot away in your wife's body. Let me remove—cut them out.

SECOND DOCTOR.   How can those mutilations cure, you cavity producer. What she needs is not excavation but reconstruction. Look at these pills, they contain wild herbs; each and every one of them have a certain duty to perform.

FIRST DOCTOR.   Ha, you—wicked disciple of the king of quacks in Peking—what is his name! The absurdity; how can poisonous mixtures containing material never found in a healthy body—cure in sickness. Listen not to him.

SECOND DOCTOR.   This fluid is a compound of condensed nutritious forces. We have made a science out of medicine. Your practice is wholly guess work. Can you explain the cause of dyridroses? Not a single organ is understood by the like of you. You simply remove them.

FOURTH DOCTOR. People should patronize a special doctor for every limb and organ. I know something that none of you know. [*Spins around like a top.*]

THIRD DOCTOR [*with a syringe*]. If you had only used the river cure. Sit in the cold water all day and let it rush through the body, comfortably, slowly, forward and backward all the time. The remedy was so getatable and so inexpensive.

FOURTH DOCTOR. By the sacred gods, what nonsense! The matter is simply this. People are starving. They stuff themselves all day and starve nevertheless. Camel's milk, that's the proper nourishment. Drink a pail or two of it, every day. Camel's milk is unreliable you say; no matter, drink it. Instead of fuel and all sorts of meat and beverages you would have simply bought a camel and milked her. It would have saved your wife the drudgery of cooking and washing china. You with proper nourishment would have been able to think twice as hard. Camel's milk, that's the solution of the universe.

FIFTH DOCTOR. Oh, my friends, how quaint all your arguments are. Human consciousness centers in the mechanism of the brain. Seem-sick's minds are machines out of order. They imagine they cannot make the body work. If your patient could be persuaded to concentrate all her thought on the one belief that she is mechanical not parasitical, she would be able to rise and dance for us, the dance of mist on the stream, just like this—

SECOND DOCTOR [*going down to the middle deck*]. Let her take one of these pills. It will chase away the evil spirits that have sneaked into her body. [*Forces a huge pill down the Wife's throat.*]

KUNG. Do what you like but don't expect any remuneration.

SECOND DOCTOR. Oh, by all the wind-imps and she dragons, it is always thus, no money to spare for absolute necessities.

FIRST DOCTOR. In this case, duty prompts to sharpen my knives.

SECOND DOCTOR. Oh, by all that is sacred, I gave her the wrong pill.

KUNG [*makes his Wife vomit the pill by thrusting his middle finger into her throat*]. Now that is enough! Get out of here bragging ninnies, all of you. You have tried my patience long enough. If you can not help her, what do you stand around here for? [*Kicks at the doctors who, jammering, scramble away.*]

SIXTH DOCTOR. I feel so sorry for you. Why did you not call me two weeks ago? I knew it was a hopeless case as soon as I saw her. I must know the entire past, breed and ancestry, manner of living, habits, diet, occupation, temperament of a patient before I can suggest a remedy. For to lay down a precise definition of disease is difficult, and we should be content with saying it is a deviation from health. Such a deviation may be called forth either by some natural defect or may be caused—

KUNG. You seem more sensible than the others, but I cannot help myself, I have to kick you out too with the rest [*Kicks at the* SIXTH DOCTOR.]

HOUSE LEEK. Fucie, Fucie, come let us have a talk together. It will be the last.

KUNG [*going down to Wife's couch*]. You said so twice before.

HOUSE LEEK. And you were probably deeply grieved that it did not happen. Well, Fucie, this time it is serious. Some unknown power haunts me. I felt it coming on since yesterday. It will break me before the day is past. [*Pause.*]

KUNG. Sweetflag, dear, where are your thoughts?

HOUSE LEEK. I search my soul tonight. I never had much of an individuality, and when I married you, I was entirely

31

absorbed by you. I liked the things you liked. My face, even my arms and legs became bony like yours and so I lived on, a weak reflection of yourself, and now when the hour has come that concerns only me, I would like to find again my original inner self, therefore I search my soul tonight. Put me into my coffin, dear. [KUNG *washes his wife's face and hands and dresses her up in her best clothes.*]

KUNG. Shall I send for a magic worker?

HOUSE LEEK. How kind of you. No, in my last moment I would like to please you. I know my foolish desire for incense and sacrifice always stood between us.

KUNG. I always admired you for remaining faithful to your belief. Everybody is free to worship existence as he pleases.

HOUSE LEEK. Tell me the truth, would it not please you just a little?

KUNG. Who can tell?

HOUSE LEEK. Then I won't have a magician.

KUNG [*aside*]. It is serious this time. Fee Fee, run call the relatives. [*Carries her upstairs and places her into the coffin.*]

HOUSE LEEK. You were always so content.

KUNG. Tried at least to be, only my colossal ideas bothered me—occasionally.

HOUSE LEEK. We have had many quarrels, hadn't we, but after all husband and wife can have no enmities as long as they sleep together. We did not always understand each other, yet we loved despite all that.

KUNG. Yes, you have been often in my way, so I have been in yours. We are all in each other's way, House Leek. Do you rest cozily now?

HOUSE LEEK. I have terrible pains. That frightful pill. All will soon be over with me.

KING. Poor Sweetflag. You have suffered a great deal—

HOUSE LEEK No matter, you always pointed out toward something higher. That I could have had with nobody else.

KUNG. I like to see the sky from horizon to horizon, and a vast expanse of water hastening toward the sea.

HOUSE LEEK. I could never see things as beautifully as you. Your songs of joyous vigor and victory, I could hardly hear in the little corner of the world in which I lived. How plainly I remember the first night on the river, when the dark sky hovered over us like a big black umbrella with a few holes through which we could see the sun. That is the way I saw life. But I always sympathized with you, tried to understand you, and you always pointed toward something higher—that I could have had with nobody else but you, Fucie. [*Dies.*]

KUNG'S MOTHER [*behind screen*]. Oh, the hardships of this life! Why, therefore?

MIDWIFE. There is a good reason for it. That is why mothers love their children. The gods managed it wisely.

KUNG'S MOTHER. The gods be damned.

KUNG. How can a human being cease to exist so suddenly! [*Puts into his Wife's mouth a milky white celadon and blood red jade stone.*] Take them with you to eternity. She liked jade stones so much. To think that she is no more, who only a moment ago still talked to me. It is absurd. Oh, that one could run away from death. Oh, this painful yearning for all that is life. Fee Fee, my sons! To feel one's own life fully, to intoxicate oneself with it, to seize every moment with a firm grasp, to sink into the glowing waters of life and to float on them forever.

KUNG'S MOTHER. I burst—midwife, I burst!

[KUNG *hastens to the staircase that leads to the lower deck and listens.*]

KUNG'S MOTHER. What is the matter with the child! What is the matter with the child!

MIDWIFE. Keep quiet. It may be a boy this time.

FEE FEE [*seated on the rat lines, sings*]. "Fish with silver scales splash in the water—"

33

KUNG'S MOTHER. Fie, fah, fum. Well?

MIDWIFE. After all, merely a girl!

KUNG. Venerable Mother, allow me to congratulate you—on your twenty-fourth offspring—

KUNG'S MOTHER [*screams*]. Twenty-fifth, you good for nothing. Will you spoil my reputation?

KUNG. Oh, what a world this is. [*Dances about.*]

HOUSE LEEK [*sitting up in the coffin*]. Fucie, Fucie, where are you? Can't you stay the last moment with me?

KUNG [*dumbfounded*]. Why, I thought you—

HOUSE LEEK. You thought I was dead. Well, I am glad to have the opportunity to see how deeply you are affected by my departure.

KUNG. Mourning is done inside—in after years.

HOUSE LEEK. Yes, it is more convenient that way. Of course, I cannot understand your love for humanity at large, you cruel tiger, dancing, because you are single again, you basilisk, ready to browse upon the first maiden that comes your way, oh my, oh my—[*Sinks back exhausted.*]

KUNG. Marry again! Once was enough. It is sufficient to have made one woman unhappy.

[FUNERAL DIRECTOR *arrives and peers into the coffin.*]

KUNG. Go home again. Why, she is still alive.

FUNERAL DIRECTOR. I see, I'll sit down and wait a bit. She won't last long.

HOUSE LEEK. Pardon me, Fucie, I was wrong. Take care of the children and think of me lovingly now and then. [*Dies.*]

RELATIVES [*enter*]. So she is really dead. Poor House Leek. Ah, we are so sorrow laden. Such an unexpected demise. The wretched female.

KUNG [*to a relative*]. Muskcollector, lend to me sufficiently to give my wife a decent burial show.

MUSKCOLLECTOR. Really, you can hardly expect that from me. I have given you so much at various occasions,

34

with no chance of ever getting it back. You remember I once gave you an entire year's rent, and you did not even thank me—you took it as if the giving of money were the most natural thing on earth.

KUNG. Money represents solely the mastery over material things.

MUSKCOLLECTOR. Nevertheless difficult to get, and honor to those who do get it.

KUNG. I never saw anything noble in money.

MUSKCOLLECTOR. But I do, that's where we differ, ink dipper.

[KUNG *steps up to another relative.*]

GRASSHOPPERHUNTER. I would like to, Kung, but if you knew how bad business has been of late. I would not hesitate a moment, but, on my honor, I cannot afford it. You two really have been careless. Have I not told your wife a hundred times to save up a few kash every week. If she had listened to my economic wisdom she could now be decently palled up.

KUNG. Save? How could she?

MUSKCOLLECTOR. I think this case concerns the entire family. A collection should be made. That is where your aloofness from common interest has led you to.

GAMBLINGHOUSEKEEPER. I must say you have treated my sister shamefully. They even say you have cudgeled her. Now is that right? I do not care how smart you are.

KUNG. Women do not understand superior or abnormal capacities. Nobody does for that matter. Genius is like a jug filled to overflowing with some boiling liquid; but no vessel—though most of them are empty enough—is held up to participate in its contents. People are afraid of getting scalded. Makers of things and thoughts may be envied, but they are worshipped by few, and those who profess to adore them are destined to suffer, because even they do not comprehend a creature going its own way.

GAMBLINGHOUSEKEEPER. Of course us poor money grabbers cannot tell parables, how to improve our personal welfare. We simply do it.

[*A Delegation of the* LADIES OF THE ORDER OF PURITY *arrive.*]

SPOKESWOMAN. Harken to us a moment—just a stray moment, grave thinker of things, illustrious and lovely man. Our minds are troubled over the abominations of the river population. We wish to cleanse the pleasure resorts of workers of iniquity, restore the waterfront to the joys of salvation, protect our populous city against transgressions in public places, and prevent the young from gazing at the uncovered limbs of shame. Love traffic must cease.

KUNG. Venerable dames, if you own any such magic as to lift crimps and pimps, harlots and sex hungry males to the plateaus of righteousness, you are entitled to even tinier hoofs than you sport now. But why not allow these windfalls to be stamped into the ground or roll into a ditch? They might prefer it to being gathered and cooked into transparent jelly. Would you yourselves care to have some official regulate the jocularities of your marital couch? [*Talks to the ladies as he walks away with them to another part of the deck.*]

GAMBLINGHOUSEKEEPER'S WIFE. Oh, how I sorrow for her. Such a life as she had led. May the gods preserve me from such a fate. She was a good, exemplary wench. I will take her fan for a keepsake.

MUSKCOLLECTOR'S WIFE. She has not even got a silver hairpin. Well, I will be satisfied with this neckerchief. [*Looks about if nobody sees her and takes neckerchief.*] It is ragged but not beyond mending.

GRASSHOPPERHUNTER. I'll keep these jade stones. They will do more good here on earth than in her mouth in eternity.

TOOTHPULLER'S WIFE. How beautiful she looks! She

was a dear little doll of a thing. I must take this jacket to remember her. Quick, lift her, pull off the trousers too. They are rather worn.

BONECARVER'S WIFE. I can make something for my youngest daughter out of them. She won't get married for some time.

COFFINPAINTER'S WIFE. The skirt will do for me. How old fashioned it looks.

GRASSHOPPERHUNTER'S WIFE. Ah, too deplorable to lose her in this fashion. She has had a hard time of it. He has never taken proper care of her, big slop that he is. Only look at the shoes on her fat feet. I know she would have given the shoes to me. Pretty far gone, still better than nothing.

BONECARVER [to his wife]. I wonder if those socks would fit you. They are lined with cotton.

COFFINPAINTER. If you all take something, I take something too. She does not need those scissors.

BONECARVER'S WIFE. A pretty good shift—not soiled either. It is of no use to the dead. So I better take it. [Pulls off shift—the upper part of corpse hangs over the edge of the coffin.] It will do for bandages.

GAMBLINGHOUSEKEEPER'S WIFE. Why, is there nothing left for me. All naked. Did you really take everything, you thieves. Quick, lend me the scissors, I'll cut off her hair. My hubbie will have the finest trailing mustache in the street.

TOOTHPULLER. I think I'll break out a few of her teeth. She won't do any more chewing, and it will come handy in my trade. This one and that one! [Breaks out a few teeth.]

SPOKESWOMAN [returning, to KUNG]. You misunderstand our mission. We lead a strictly moral life. If temptation approaches us we carefully avoid it.

KUNG. Never stopped a man's roaming hand, aye?

LADIES [scream]. Oh, he is violating our purity! He has stabbed the consciousness of our religious sentiment. [Exit.]

KUNG. How I would like to empty some cess-pool on

37

their immaculate frocks! [*Steps up to the coffin.*] What is this! Who has dared to profane the dead! Oh, you vile mob! Dregs of all created things! There exists nothing in the world for you but your monstrous greed, nothing but to satisfy your low instincts of gain. You know of no joy except robbing each other, and no sorrow except losing some of your paltry possessions. [*Searches relatives with a stick; they scream and sneak away.*] And you poor woman—[*to* FUNERAL DIRECTOR] Why did you not prevent it?

FUNERAL DIRECTOR.   That is not my business.

KUNG.   Then take yourself hence. There will be no funeral. [*In despairing love takes the corpse into his arms, and doing so, he slips and falls, and the corpse rolls along the deck and overboard.*] The monsters of the deep will treat you more kindly than the vermin that infests this earth. Float down to the sea. Farewell. [*Looks at the sky.*] Shadows, clouds, mist and spume, that is what we know of a future state.

[*The Scenery becomes formless like a Prehistoric Landscape.* KUNG, *feeling the growth of hair on his legs, stares into the gloom. Sky and river magic.*]

KUNG [*sits down, self-absorbed and ruminating, on a huge Ming Jar*].   Human beings are but insects that stick to earth as once to Pwenku's body. Life is one continuous renunciation. As we shift along, we drop one thing after the other. Fancies, hopes, ideals, the use of our senses, one after the other fall away. And the last renunciation—death.

RIVER POLICEMAN [*on the outside of* KUNG'S *houseboat, stretches forth his hand*].   Hand over what little you can spare, or I'll have to arrest you for throwing something into the river.

KUNG.   I have nothing. The worthy relatives have taken everything.

RIVER POLICEMAN.   How about the coffin then; I think it will fit my wife.

KUNG.   Take it. Be off with it.

[*An Embassy from the Highest Sovereign Court of Civil Employments enters. Two* MANDARINS *in yellow jackets— Torchlight. The relatives crouch timidly and curiously in the distance.*]

FIRST MANDARIN. Where is Confucius?

FO PA. He is sitting on the Ming over there, your Excellency.

SECOND MANDARIN. Why, he wears a yellow robe. What next!

FIRST MANDARIN. I have great news to impart to you, Kung.

KUNG [*grumbling*]. Keep them to yourself.

MUSKCOLLECTOR. He is out of his wits, your Excellency. His wife died just a few moments ago.

SECOND MANDARIN. Nevertheless, he should rise.

FIRST MANDARIN. The news I have to impart would lighten the darkest hour.

RELATIVES. Tell him, your Excellency.

FIRST MANDARIN. The Empress, who has heard of your fame and your greatness as one of the sages of our time, has conferred upon you by personal verbal order the honor and position of the Keeper of Archives of the Royal State of Chow.

KUNG. I wish House Leek could hear this. It was one of her dearest wishes. Very exceptional of you—

FIRST MANDARIN. Quick, get ready and pay your respects to the Emperor. He wishes to see you.

KUNG. Not just now.

FIRST MANDARIN. What next! Did I hear right! Do you understand me. Of course, you are as moonstruck at your unexpected luck. Let me tell you how it came about. The Emperor heard of your name. Why does he not seek any favors from me, he asked. And I answered: After having done a great deed, he like a truly great soul, conceals it and returns to his ashes, sits idly by the fireside, ragged, misunderstood, until the time for final recognition, when rags and dirt fall off. Was I not clever in putting it that way? Hey, answer us. [*Pokes* KUNG *with his umbrella.*]

KUNG. What, are you here, yet? I thought you had vanished long ago.

SECOND MANDARIN. What audacity! And still sitting on the vase!

FIRST MANDARIN. Fellow, how do you come to wear the yellow robe?

KUNG. Oh, it turned yellow from long usage. The babies did it.

SECOND MANDARIN. Are you at least ready to accompany me?

KUNG. No, not just now, if I go at all.

MEE NANG [*triumphantly*]. How he opposes the government. Greatest of all fathers!

FIRST MANDARIN. What next! Is it possible—you really insist? Are you obsessed by evil spirits?

KUNG. Not that I know of. We are all more or less obsessed by one thing or another.

FO PA. Why don't you come, then?

KUNG. Simply because I don't care to. Must there be a reason for everything?

SECOND MANDARIN. Do you know the law? A person who shall be found guilty of scoffing or showing manifest disrespect or open disobedience to an Imperial order, may be punished with the deprivation of all civil rights and exile for life to the remotest parts of the Mongolian Desert.

KUNG [*rises*]. Is that all?

FIRST MANDARIN. At last, he has risen to pay proper respects—

KUNG. I have finished, that's all. And what is your business?

[MIDWIFE *rushes across stage with the afterbirth in an urn. Some rice farmers grapple and fight for it.*]

40

FIRST MANDARIN.   He is going too far! Arrest him!

SECOND MANDARIN.   Give him one hundred strokes on his footsoles first!

FIRST MANDARIN.   A pleasant errand this. Let's adjourn, there is nothing else to do.

MEE NANG.   Now the supreme moment has come! [*Throws stinkpot; it smokes, but does not explode.*]

SECOND MANDARIN.   The Gods help us, we are among the Free Men. Soldiers, imprison everybody.

FIRST MANDARIN.   What next! And won't the Emperor be mad!

[SOLDIERS *tie* KUNG *and* MEE NANG *with ropes.*]

SECOND MANDARIN.   And hang that young fellow.

KUNG.   Clotpoll, I am ashamed of you—lynched by the government. Should we meet in the beyond, we will have a talk about this foolishness.

[SOLDIERS *lead* MEE NANG *away. Some of the* FREE MEN *try to rescue* MEE NANG, *others* KUNG.]

KUNG.   I am as free in ropes as out of them. Do not bother about me. Go, tell my pupils that they come to the prison, and there shall they see me.

CURTAIN

ACT II

Scene I. The Imperial Palace

SCENE: *The* EMPEROR'S *Study, decorated in turquoise, azurine, and dull gold. Through trellis work, overgrown with climbing plants in bloom, view on a park. Yellow Sunset with heavy purple clouds broken with the white of vivid lightning. Music is wafted in.*

THE EMPEROR [*resting on a keng with papers, jasper flute, pen, and snuff bottle scattered about him. Dress and appendages in different shades of yellow*].   The Imperial Gazette annoys me. Everything written to please me. [*Seizes jasper flute.*] Poor jasper stick, why did they disturb your dull smoothness with these stops. Four stupid tones! Why could there not be a scale of infinite length! [*Leaning back.*] These cushions stuffed with maidens' down are rather comfortable. Pshaw, to think what music could be, could we hear sounds within a sound. No doubt, they are too fugitive for our ears. Yet, waves of tone there must be that sweep unheard through space—and if they could be inflated at will with my emotions and be made responsive to all demands of imaginative thought, then music would be limitless—the chords of nature subdued to laws of harmony. [*A new coat is offered to him and he changes his dress with the help of an attendant.*] What a fragile yellow! The untrained eye would fail to discern any difference between these two.

FIRST SECRETARY.   Hallowed Majesty, the Minister of

42

Agriculture of the First Division of the Financial Court, most humbly requests an audience. Whether an extra tax should be raised on the rice crop of this year.

THE EMPEROR. Bah! Let him wait until Confucius comes.

SECOND SECRETARY. Glorious Prince, superhuman and infallible, the Minister of the Supreme Court of War most urgently requests to be granted an interview. Another battle with the Tartars is lost.

THE EMPEROR. Humph! Let him wait until Confucius comes. No more State business will be attended to until Confucius comes.

FIRST SECRETARY. And the petitions, Great Unseen. Yesterday you refused them all?

THE EMPEROR. Give them one-half for what they ask. [*Spits into* SECRETARY'S *face.*] What a bother it is to be an Emperor.

SECOND SECRETARY. Illustrious Director of the People, the ante-chambers are crowded with audience seekers, who wish to pay their respects to the Sun of Heaven.

THE EMPEROR. No audiences today.

THIRD SECRETARY [*steps up*]. Supreme Ruler, on the day after tomorrow the Annual Procession of Pregnant Women will take place.

THE EMPEROR. Ahem! I will look at them through the perforated screen as they march through the streets, their stiff voluptuous breasts and nude palpitating bellies bulging forth to glorify maternity. Flowers and streamers of colored silk shall be thrown in their way, and the crowd along the route shall prostrate itself before marching motherhood.

What a pleasure it will be to meet Confucius. Artists produce the beautiful. Such a man must in himself personify art. I would rather gaze at the shoulder of such a man than to realize the essence of a woman's beauty or the wisdom of hundreds of ordinary mandarins. My position is so exalted, my taste so rare, that only few mortals can be on equal terms with me. It is sad to be alone in this wide world. I am still too young for monotony. Perhaps the lightnings of his thought will break the yellowish brown seclusion of my life.

We will walk together over the meadows enameled with flowers, and gaze at the liquid pearls with which the sun adorns the morning. We will rest in the jade pavilions scattered at random about the hills, rising one above the other, half-hidden in tufted bamboo groves to which the sun rays never penetrate, and tired of pondering over strange jewelled sentences in his books, we will seize a flute and challenge the birds to rivalry.

[*The* DOWAGER EMPRESS *and young* EMPRESS *enter in Palaquins.*]

THE EMPRESS.   Ah, Empie, [*pouts*] you should know I am in great distress. I do not know what pantalettes I shall select for wear this afternoon. And I must decide soon so that they may be heated. [*Waves her hand as she is carried from the room.*]

THE DOWAGER EMPRESS.   You look stupid, my son.

THE EMPEROR.   Ahem! In all these ceremonies, this state business of the largest empire, often for days, for weeks, I lose myself, I become a mere machine, not noticing even the subtle changes in my morning or evening moods. I wish to widen my horizon line. I, the Son of Heaven, to whom every thing belongs beneath the sky—I, whose body is sacred and never seen by ordinary mortals, I may kneel in my temples and go through the same ceremonies as my ancestors have done for thousands of years, I may roam lonesome through my gardens of rocks of glass and ponds of colored water, but the tumult of life, my millions of subjects, my eyes have never seen, except through a perforated screen. I do not know what life is, what humanity is, what the sea and the great world outside are.

THE DOWAGER EMPRESS. Do not let that distress you, my son, it is a foolish knowledge. But let me tell you, lest I forget, a supply of fair Manchuria maidens has arrived. They have been duly washed in wine and cocoanut milk. They are ready for inspection right behind the curtain. [*Exit.*]

THE EMPEROR [*beckons; the females are led in. The* EMPER-OR *examines them in the nonchalant way of a connoisseur*]. Those breasts are well set. A good bend of arm—perhaps it was merely the light breeze which raised her wide sleeve. She is of gentle outline and dainty hue. You should have some of your teeth pulled and teeth of emerald inserted instead. They would match the color of your lips. They seem to be in good order. This maiden is like a sunflower newly washed with rain. Her hair is like cobweb of the black spiders. I wonder to what degree her passion may be made to climb. [*Shrugs his shoulders.*] That will do. Let them live in the grottoes near the lily pond, and at my first approach let them float amid the scarlet flowers like swans on a sapphire sea when the setting sun is kissing it. By and by, distribute my old set of concubines among my ministers as souvenirs, and let a shower of rose petals fall upon them as they leave the palace gates. [*In afterthought.*] After all what will it amount to! Will I ever have as much fun again as with the fei with whom I studied the passions previous to my marriage! [*Chuckles.*]

FIRST SECRETARY. The artists—

THE EMPEROR [*beckons*]. Do not bring the screen. I like to see them face to face. I would rather exclude the mandarins.

[*The* ARTISTS *enter and prostrate themselves on the ground, kneeling and knocking their heads against the floor.*]

THE EMPEROR. Rise! [*To* FIRST PAINTER.] Paint my portrait from memory, half life-size, a three-quarter back view.

FIRST PAINTER [*stammers*].   A back view!

THE EMPEROR.   You enjoy the reputation of showing great power in the interpretation of character, yes, express my character in the outward appearance of my back. [*To* FIRST ARTIST-ARTISAN.] You are the man who has worked over twenty years on the ornamentation of a doorway with metallic sculpture. The Minister of Art will send you a block of spotless chrysoprase of Khotan, as big as my body; carve a dragon, make it perfect, even if it should take you the rest of your life. You shall be in need of nothing. [*To* SECOND PAINTER.] The picture you have painted is abominable. It is worse than bad, it is pretty, you tumbledung! [*Slaps him in the face.*] Let him be removed for ten years to the utmost wilds of Tartary. There in the solitude you may learn to paint. Consider me lenient too, for the lechery of Art is more disgusting than that of the body. A guttersnipe is a seraphim in comparison with you. [*To* SECOND ARTIST-ARTISAN.] You have constructed a new pipe. Make him a Mandarin! He has given pleasure to thousands by tranforming a simple utensil into a work of art. [*To* FIRST ARCHITECT.] You want to build a pai-loo, for whom?

FIRST ARCHITECT.   Hallowed Majesty, for my native village Tchi. As pagodas are supposed to effect a fall of rain upon the surrounding country as far as the eye can discern their painted top—we have had very bad crops of late, and need a fertilizing influence.

THE EMPEROR.   The old superstitions seem to you a welcome instrument to enrich yourself! Leave that to the rain-makers. Not granted. [*To* SECOND ARCHITECT.] And you—

SECOND ARCHITECT.   Serene Highness, to build a pai-fong for a woman whose loins remained unfurrowed until she was thirty, whereupon she gave birth to one healthy child annually for fifteen years, after which period her husband died and she entered a second state of virginity until her death.

THE EMPEROR. Granted. [*To* FIRST LANDSCAPE GARDENER.] How is the labyrinthian rockery on the Dragon Mount? Hurry with it, so that my grandchildren may see it finished. Make the roads like the thoughts of our mind. We never know where they are leading to. And bronze the rocks along the banks of the river, so that its sluggish greenish flood may resemble an emerald serpent set in gold. Only red fish shall sport in its waters. [*To* SECOND LANDSCAPE GARDENER.] How is my kiosque in the Summer Palace of Colored Majolica? Make it a pleasant retreat in summer for those of lazy philosophic taste, who enjoy musing on life's changes and study human nature as it hurries and bustles below. Plant the black mud on the graceful, many-gabled roofs with seeds, so that they may take root and spring up in summer, covering the roof with splashes of warm verdure. [*To* THIRD LANDSCAPE GARDENER.] You are the new landscape gardener of my Autumn Palace. Yes, I was greatly displeased with the last one. He had no eye for the deep, subdued, reticent charms of nature, when the wild roses glow no longer, when the cuckoo's frolicsome call has ceased, and the foliage falls in that indefinable language of rustling sounds which the human mind cannot follow, and art not reflect. Combine the yellow, reds and blacks, the bronzen foliage of the mahogany, the violet hues of the storax and the golden leaves of the snowball tree into some picture, and let sunlight filtering through, lend them an inner life which paintings generally lack. Paint me before some window a picture of the evergreen of hoary oaks, the deepening dusk of soaring cypresses, broken by lines of white barked fir and red-leafed iron wood, and behind them a vista of undulating fields that change their color softly from emerald to amethyst.

[*To* MASTER OF CEREMONIES.] Let the dancing women tonight be dressed in yellow, white and gold, and with lanterns in ever-changing dreams of circle, square, and star reveal the rhythmic book of form. White lanterns only!

[*To* FIREWORKER.]   Shall I also tire of my favorite art!
Paint me more radiant scenes upon the canvas of the sky
than dragons unrolling their tails, galloping cavalcades of
horses, colored ribbons flying in the wind, and giant eagles
changing into flights of monoliths, across turbulent dark
grey seas, desolate twilight plains, pigeons fluttering down-
ward. Fireworks should be shown from high or the skylines
of large cities. Make me some fiery bush whose fire leaves
crawl over the surface of the earth and blossoming forth into
a million flower-sparks, grow and grow in soaring luminous
lines into the glowing trunks of trees. Then let a wind
wrapped in some white cloud sweep through the forest fire,
let the vibrant foliage shed a spray of many-colored buds, a
rain of incandescent fire-fruit; and finally let a hurricane
uproot these burning trees, hurl them into air and scatter
them across the dark blue distances of night. And from the
balcony that overlooks the Yellow River's embouchure, I
fain would see a long procession of giant lantern-lighted
gondolas with looming pagodas of luminous jewelry, whose
color flares would flush the skies with vibrant hieroglyphics, gliding down the river in a scintillant serpent line
to drown their dreams of fire in the sea.

   [*To* COOK.]   I read your book on the ethics of cooking. It is
exquisite. I enjoyed your treatise on how to prepare peacock
comb, how to fry silk worms, and pickle shark fin; also your
new method of stewing duck tongues with bamboo sprouts.
If your practice equals your theories—can you cut a pigeon's
kidney into an open flower and give to each petal a different
flavor, and stain caterpillars red so that they look like the
lips of an amorous woman?

   COOK [*has nodded solemnly to every question, presents his
attendants*].   Wisdom and virtue of the nation, look how
clean their fingernails are! They do not perspire, snuff with
moderation, nor do they poke at their bodies; they have no
bad habits soever. Allow me to serve you something cool and
refreshing in silver, blue and grey.

THE EMPEROR. Ah, a dumpling with a bitter-sweet surprise inside. Very tasty. A pretty notion, that of yours, to satisfy all senses at once time, with ever-varying subtleties of harmony. The appearance of food—[COOK *wants to interrupt him.*] You may speak.

COOK. I would like to introduce a greater variety of form in the presentation of food, oh, Son of Heaven. Did you notice my chapter on the ways of cutting meat and vegetables into peculiar figures of varying sizes?

THE EMPEROR [*nods*]. I am tired of my ivory gold-tipped eating sticks—try some with handles of silver filigree set with pearls—also of those white dishes with dark blue ornaments, although I realize that they lend grace, in particular to emerald, red and yellow food.

COOK. I would humbly suggest for state dinners, when only a stickfull of everything is taken, and often spat out again, plates with colored elevations. For a dark green soup a plate with orange tips, shimmering through the sombre brew—

THE EMPEROR. Order a set for the next hundred course dinner. [*Yawns.*]

COOK. Then the odor, Just, True and Great One! The special aroma of the food should be used as the leading theme and complementary odors added. Game with a healthful balsam of fir and pine cone. Fish with a whiff of the brine and the rottening seaweed on the shore. The perfumes to be distributed by the burning of smokeless powders carried by air-currents, while fans would gently remove the lingering scent before the next course is served. The palate should be kept sensitive by changing constantly the grain, solidity and temperature of each dish, from heavy dullness to sparkling light, from snowy chillness to the heat of desert sands. And the music accompanying the courses should harmonize with the quality of the food. With bird nest's soup a slow gliding measure; with hard cakes of cranberry jelly which have to be broken a certain dancing graceful rhythm; fowl in the nest with sparkling rhythms.

THE EMPEROR. You talk too much. Better stuff your melons! Go! Join the Imperial Assembly of Expert Cooks that sits in council every evening to provide for my next month's meals. [*Makes a gesture.*]

MASTER OF CEREMONIES [*shouts*]. All present are asked to make use of the castle gate!

THE EMPEROR. All this is meaningless. Man is so forgetful. What do we remember of looking at a carved camel, a play, or of having an amorous tussle with a Tartar wench! Merely an impression of color, a few attitudes, bites and kisses, the rest is forgotten. And just as forgetful as man are nations. The possessions of the day, the tools of culture, by some change, will cease to exist and be invented anew, perchance, after thousands of years. [*To* MANDARINS *who enter.*] You come from the old rind-plugger Confucius! Where is he?

FIRST MANDARIN. Great Unseen! Heaven's Vice Regent here below, I do not know how to communicate to your serene aural sense the audacity of the Man from the Yellow River.

THE EMPEROR [*scratching his ear with thumb and little finger*]. Well go on—

SECOND MANDARIN. He—no, I must have lost my wits, I can not persuade myself that it is really true—he refused— to come to see the sun—

THE EMPEROR. Refused to see me? Impossible. I am the Emperor.

[*Mandarins and all attendants throw themselves prostrate on the floor.*]

THE EMPEROR [*overcome with momentary awe*]. The first man whom I wish to see and he refuses to see me. That is colossal, that man has character. Whatever you have done with him, set him free, at once! I shall go to see him.

THE EMPRESS [*enters in palaquin*]. I have selected panta-

50

lettes for this afternoon, Empie, a pair of green embroidered with red, reminding me of heliotropes, but alas I am in the same dilemma now, I do not know what pair I shall wear this evening. And no doubt, we have to make concessions to the Tartars, which means a change in my allowances.

CURTAIN

ACT II

Scene II. A Prison

SCENE: *A large Cell with moist walls and dirty water dripping through the ceiling. Through the Iron Bars one can see the Prison Yard. Rats are running to and fro on the rottening straw.*

To the right KUNG, KANG, *the* PRINCE OF THIEVES *and other prisoners squat on the foul floor.*

KUNG [*conversing through the bars with* FO PA *and a* RICH MERCHANT]. It is not the first time I am here.

RICH MERCHANT. Deign to accept it after all, do.

FO PA. It is of no avail. I know him. Surely by offering him to pawn my jewels I did all that I can afford to do. Look at his big carnelian.

RICH MERCHANT. What's to be done! It hurts me to see him suffer, the man who glorified my native kingdom Lou.

KUNG. I have never been used to much luxury.

FO PA. Surely, you do not find this a place that lends wings to the soul!

KUNG [*laughs*]. Food and shelter are atrocious, the company rather interesting.

RICH MERCHANT. Illusions! I think you have seen enough of it by this time. Why do you refuse to accept my offer? Nobody has more right to my money than you. I like men who know what I don't know.

[*A Prisoner is led by very courteously.*]

KUNG. What impressionistic promenade is he indulging in?

JAILER. He has rented a private pavilion, furnished.

RICH MERCHANT. Can Kung have the same accommodations?

JAILER. For money you can have anything within these walls.

KUNG. You can buy justice; the more money you spend, the bigger a slice of justice you can get.

JAILER. We adjust matters by the month. If you can pay one hundred, we can give you a furnished pavilion with board and use of swimming pool and library, you wouldn't be put up better in a caravansary. If you can pay two hundred, we allow you to have a key, and you can stroll about the prison park, the pleasure grounds and gambling pagodas attached to the institution. Should you desire to keep a mistress with painted lips, it will cost you one thousand and extra board for her. You may invite friends, give dinner parties, and from time to time, should your inclination run that way, spend a day or so outside of prison, of course accompanied by a jailer in civilian garb. This would amount to two thousand. Whereas for ten thousand we close our eyes and forget to lock the gate. Think it over. [*Exit.*]

KUNG. A beautiful system to establish law and justice in the land.

RICH MERCHANT. Now look, only ten thousand to get you out of this vile place. I won't miss it at all.

FO PA. You can't persuade a goat. Let us go. [*Yawns.*] The domain of sleep demands my immediate attention.

RICH MERCHANT. Really, you anger me. I traveled all this way specially for the purpose, and nothing is accomplished.

KUNG. You seem to think of your own pleasure after all more than mine. That's right.

RICH MERCHANT. You won't accept my offer then?

KUNG. If I had no family, I might.

RICH MERCHANT. What can they do?

KUNG. Everything I need.

RICH MERCHANT. You prefer to stay imprisoned?

KUNG. I do not consider myself imprisoned, I came here willingly.

RICH MERCHANT. Oh, your thoughts are out of gear. I won't come again, I assure you. [*Turns to exit, looks back once more.*] Let me at least send you a counselor.

KUNG. I need nobody to disguise matters for me. I shall plead my own cause. I salute you. [FO PA *and* RICH MERCHANT *exit.*] What is the good of laws couched in terms that even men of learning, without special professional reasoning, fail to comprehend. Mole-work!

JAILER [*returns*]. Well, will the sparrows feed their young?

KUNG. Who can tell! Abalones have to boil three days, you know.

[*Several barrels of wine are rolled through the corridor.*]

JAILER. They will see to it, sly rascal, eh. [*Poking at him through the bars.*] Do you want some of the yellow stuff? What, not even enough for that. Why didn't you say so. Keeping me here all the time. I must say, you got yourself into a nice scrape. [*Exit.*]

KUNG. State officials seem to know no shame. They sit in costly halls, ride fine steeds, drink themselves drunk and stuff themselves with the richest fare. Even to the criminal their awe-inspiring mien decays as law itself. All gold and gems without and rotten cocoons within. An honest citizen's prayer should be by night and day, "Give us a pure civil government!"

[*In the prison yard an Orgy of male and female prisoners, drunk and in indecent exposure, takes place.*]

ONE OF THE PRISONERS. Who is the woman who feasts so lavishly?

PRINCE OF THIEVES. Don't you know The Bloody Marquise? How can one be so ignorant of the annals of contemporary crime. You are not in love with your profession. Within five years she has lured more than five hundred maidens into her service and beaten them to death. Her victims, naked and tied, furnished to her delicious music by their shrieks and groans. With ecstasy she feasted her eyes on the convulsions. She laughed with joy when their warm blood sprinkled red flowers upon her dress. Deprived of pity, she was interested only in watching the moment when the soul left the tormented body. Condemned to death—by powerful influence, as she is a Daughter of the Revolution—her sentence was changed into imprisonment for life. As she is wealthy, she has a gay time of it, although the pleasure of watching souls leave their bodies is no longer hers.

KUNG. I wonder whether she is pious.

KANG [*with crushed ankles*]. She is a superior artist. I am in for twenty-nine assaults upon noblemen's daughters. I killed only half a dozen, or maybe seven!

PRINCE OF THIEVES. It will fare hard with you.

KANG. Pish! Nobody can be sentenced who has not confessed his guilt.

PRINCE OF THIEVES. They will torture you, crush your body as they crushed your ankles.

KANG. Then I'll hum a melody as my illustrious father did, when they tore out the peccant parts of his body with fiery pincers.

PRINCE OF THIEVES. Was that your father? He was a hero indeed. I would like to help you. You know I am the Prince of Thieves—sentenced twelve times, evaded sentence more than fifty times, escaped from prison three times—the son of one of the most celebrated crooks of the empire, and the associate of all famous criminals. I never refuse to help a pal. I have devoted almost the entire product of my labors to the support of the wives and children of my professional acquaintances in bad luck.

KANG. I am too sentimental. How could they have caught me, had I not returned to my lodging. I kept a little cricket in a bamboo cage, and was afraid it would starve to death. Besides it had to be taken out for a walk.

[*Another prisoner is pushed in.*]

PRISONERS. What are you in for, Number Five?

CHILD MURDERER. Ah, much noise about nothing. Last June, when the gopher of my wife died, I went to live with another womb-man, and my child seemed to be in the way. So I killed it.

JAILER. Yes, he pitched the infant into some heap of rubbish, and when it cried from hunger or cold, he—[*Makes a gesture.*]

CHILD MURDERER. It had a lot of vitality for so small a thing.

JAILER. A black poodle was the baby's only friend. He came to lick the sores. [*Exit.*]

PRINCE OF THIEVES. You are a scoundrel.

CHILD MURDERER [*shrugs his shoulders*]. How so! The child was dirty and deserved punishment.

PRINCE OF THIEVES. Even unto death! [*They all turn away from him.*]

CHILD MURDERER. I didn't mean to kill it particularly. I struck it in the back with a knife occasionally because other punishments had no effect. A stick was useless. I had to give up using an iron rod. Pooh, it drove me wild, and when I am mad, I go too far, perhaps. For instance, one day when it had angered me, I— It was its own fault. Why did it make me desperate. [*To returning* JAILER *accompanied by* GAMBLING-HOUSEKEEPER.] Get me some wine.

JAILER. Oh, you have money. I did not know. Number five may move about more freely. Go along.

GAMBLINGHOUSEKEEPER [*to* PRINCE OF THIEVES]. Are you ready to leave? I paid for you. [*Looks at* KUNG *with a shoulder shrug.*] We cannot get along without you. You are so phenomenally clever with your middle finger.

PRINCE OF THIEVES. Thanks. You restore my belief in my profession. For it was a trifle hard after doing a lot of lifting for others, a pal should have played me false. He can't be much good, he will die in the gutter. Farewell, gentlemen, I shall remember your case, Kang. I am also sorry for you, Kung. You seem to be a decent sort of a fellow, tho' I have not much use for scribblers.

KUNG. Who can tell! My relatives have children or somebody else to take care of, so I cannot accept any help from them. One of my sons joined the Order of Ugliness. My other son has been hung for amusing himself with a stink-pot. My daughter may find some way—

PRINCE OF THIEVES. Is she a handsome lass? Virgin, perchance?

KUNG. Who can tell! Fathers do not always know.

PRINCE OF THIEVES. Give her my address. Should I like her—she does not look too much like you, does she—and she is willing to trade, I may be tempted to set you free. [*Exit with* JAILER *and* GAMBLINGHOUSEKEEPER.]

KUNG [*grins—in deep meditation*]. What mankind needs most is a new code of law, written in plain language in a few thousand words, intelligible to all. —I often thought of it, but can one man cook a soup that would prove tasty to all! Probably not. One can make suggestions merely. —Yet, laws there must be as men are more cunning and presumptuous than beasts. We are all tainted like rotten fruit. Human shortcomings are like weeds, one never gets through cutting them.

To promulgate justice in this land, for witness, plaintiff and defendant alike, capital punishment should be abolished, except in convictions for bribery of officials concerned in the execution of the law. The machinery of the law should be clean, run as smoothly as a rich man's garden

57

party. No crime can be more atrocious than the dishonesty of an official who has been chosen to protect the community. —All witnesses should be tested as to the trustworthiness of their testimony, and after each trial all incidents suspicious of perjury should be taken up without delay and dealt with most severely. —A constable who neglects to perform a mission of state, any one who utters threats against a witness, or harbors a fugitive and refuses to produce him should be subject to drastic penalties.

For all offences, the severest punishment should be imprisonment for twenty years, excepting for murder; life takers should be imprisoned for life as one is never sure that they may not make a habit of killing. People acquitted of murder should remain under suspicion. We never know whom our sweethearts kiss.

Prisons should be changed into work houses and convict farms, with strict and frugal but humane and sanitary treatment, and with a separate system for the nights. Criminals are the sick children of society. In the work-houses, they will work at their trade or profession; if they have none, they will be forced to acquire one. With their earnings they will pay what a prisoner costs the state. With the remainder, if not due to somebody else, they may buy snuff or dried watermelon seeds, support their family, or they may save it, which savings will be handed to them with interest when they are discharged. And as they leave the prison, they will be re-instated in society. Still, is it not quaint that a certain time limit should expiate a crime, that a guilty person may be dishonored for five years and after that again be as good or bad as anybody else.

These are the insufficiencies of man-made justice, and yet existence would be rather cumbersome without the repression of theft, for instance. We like to keep the truck we have; thus highwaymen and burglars, caught in the act, may suffer death, if left to the mercy of the mob. Not much harm done, as little as if a man who set fire to a house were thrown into the flames and burnt. And yet what is man's property but an accumulation at the expense of others. Were it not best if a thief that has stolen an ox, sheep, pig, ass or camel, or any article of value, should be asked merely to restore it to the owner, and only in case he cannot do this be sentenced to half a year or a good flogging, and forced to work off the damage he has done to the plaintiff! —He will be free, though under surveillance of the state, and only in case he finds no way of squaring his debt, be sent to the workhouse. This would do away with punishing people for having stolen a dish of rice. The heartless wretch who refuses food to a starving being should be punished as severely as the receiver of stolen goods, no, not quite as stringently.

If a child of age, in rage or intentionally strikes its parents, the child should be starved until too weak to strike again. If a person causes by mere accident the loss or use of another person's eye, or organ, he shall answer for the doctor and be obliged to pay a pension to the crippled person for the rest of his or the victim's life according to the severity of the injury.

If a man strikes a woman so that she miscarries, he shall maintain her for life, but if the woman dies, he shall be imprisoned for life. Life is the only thing that can not be replaced and he who takes it should suffer, not by taking his however. Death in itself is no punishment; hard labor, privation and fear of death are. Thus should it fare with a contractor whose house fell upon some inmate of the house and killed him; if no life is lost the builder must rebuild the house at his own cost. A party who wrecks a ship which he hires should render ship for ship to the boatman.

Also the law as to desertion should be clear. The wife of a man who deserts her should be free to marry again, nor should the husband on his return be able to compel her to share couch and food with him. If a man wishes to put away his wife or concubine who has borne him children, because she has set her face to go forth, acted the fool and wasted his house, he shall nevertheless give her sufficient means to live and to bring up her children, unless he take care of them himself. If a childless wife is put away for similar reasons, he shall give her enough money to repay the years she wasted with him until she marries another ploughman of her choice. And the wife may divorce her husband if she hates him and says "Thou shalt not possess me" providing she can prove that she has been economical and had no open vice, and if her husband has gone out in wantonness and greatly belittled her; in that case she is entitled to freedom and temporary support. The children must be supported, and women sacrifice too much by entering the nuptial state that they can venture forth anew into life without a supply of socks and bellybands. The best way out of it would be if both parties would come to an agreement that would cover their individual relations and then strictly live up to their self-made obligation.

Debts over two years standing should be paid off in the workhouse. Honesty should be enforced. This would be decidedly at my expense. I would have to spend considerable stretches of my life within the workhouse.

Drunkards, with the tingle of rosewine in their veins and loafers, abusers of the fresh air habit, whenever they become a nuisance should be deprived of the causes of their misconduct and be put under medical care. —If a man commits rape, without doing actual injury to the person, he should simply be beaten green and purple and an official prostitute be sent to him. The emperor, who can choose from all women over twelve, will never assault a farmer's daughter on the highway.

Nobody should be punished except he or she directly injures another member of the community. Not indirectly, for then all of us would march together to the workhouse. —Unnatural habits have always remained a mystery to me. As long as the practitioners of such sex expression molest only others similarly inclined, their queer exploitations and ecstasies should not be punishable. Rather those childless women who constantly pester men—who openly flaunt their danger zone but allow no trespassing—their bodies should be forced to serve some—no that would be wrong too. One can do with one's body whatever one pleases.

To prohibit suicide by chewing gold leaves is an absurdity. If one has a right of possession to anything at all, one has a right to one's soul, it is so elusive. However, one has no right to cause troubles to the community. The bunglers, who merely attempt suicide, should pay the expenses of the trouble their cowardice and false pathos cause the community; medical service, reviving processes, injections and so forth.

If a man is the sole seducer of a young girl, he ought to be obliged either to marry her or to pay one half of the child's expenses. In all cases pertaining to womanhood, half of the jury should consist of women—ah, there are so many things to think of!

The accumulation of wealth beyond a certain liberal sufficiency should be made so cumbersome that nobody would care to be an exploiter of his brothermen. Furthermore, money should not be inheritable, a small amount perhaps—only land, the old homestead, personal belongings.

There should be no sick houses, merely emergency booths, as few public institutions as possible. The good will of the people, of one being to another, should take the place. There is no room for municipal charity among real men.

[FEE FEE *enters.*]

KUNG. Ah my daughter, so spick and span, what sort of news do you bring?

FEE FEE. I have found a way to help you, venerable father.

KUNG. That sounds pleasant to my ears, like a rhythm of four on a wire harmonica.

FEE FEE. I shall offer my body to some rich man. Do you approve of it? I will deck myself out in my choicest attire, prepare my body by the most approved methods of washing, kneading and perfuming, put two beauty spots on my temples and a red dot on the middle of my lips. I will adorn my hair with the loveliest of flowers, and by every device in my power influence some noblemen's heart to inordinate love, and if I succeed in so doing and we are hugger-mugging together, I will make him comply with my desire to set you free.

KUNG. Have I the right to accept this sacrifice? Have I been a good father to you?

FEE FEE. You have always done your duty towards me, now I will do my duty towards you.

KUNG. Then go and do as you say, flapper dear.

FEE FEE. Am I beautiful enough to entice a man?

KUNG. Who can tell! Every woman is resistless to one man or another, and can turn him into an ass or swine. But no use of teaching a monkey to climb a tree. I can give you the address of the Prince of Thieves.

CURTAIN

ACT II

Scene III. In the Famine District

SCENE: *A ravine. Only a few feet from the proscenium, a straight wall of rock forms the background. At the bottom of the wall some leafless shrubbery and a clump of gnarled and knotted trees without foliage, all covered with dust. The rocks are so high that the spectators can see only the feet of people who pass on the top of the plateau. A few human bones glisten and crack in the lazy heat.*

Villagers, showing different stages of starvation, crawl along the pass like wild animals. An old naked woman, withered to a skeleton, with scrawny neck scarce strong enough to hold her head, in which the eyeballs rot away, gnaws desperately at the bark of a tree. A man, his fleshless lips, shrinking back from his teeth, staggers with ulcered feet enveloped in black clouds of flies across the stage and stabs himself; his wife, children and other villagers fall like vultures upon him to lick his blood but his wasted body scarcely bleeds. A young mother, with eyes glimmering like jewels in their hollow sockets, her hands and feet eaten away by leprosy, throttles her baby whose limbs have shriveled into stumps, and in her hopeless frenzy beats a melody on the distended, drumlike belly of the child.

KUNG [*sits in the foreground to the left, groping into the dry, hot sand, and letting it flow through his fingers*]. Here help is useless. They no longer know human speech. Here people that deem themselves unfortunate in the ordinary ways of life could learn what suffering means. —Strange, how even

63

in the utmost misery, a human being clings to life. They have swallowed their own water, gnawed at their own bones and that of corpses. How foolish to make so much of life! Rather worship death; alas, that is difficult. We rather prefer to be nothing than not to be at all.

[*The Imperial Caravan arrives on the plateau, only the feet of the camels and the retinue are visible to the audience. The* EMPEROR *is carried—from the right into the pass—in a palaquin of ebony and gold orange cushions, accompanied by* MAN- DARINS, *and warriors in scale armor of black copper.*]

THE EMPEROR.   So this is the way people look when they do not eat or drink. It is like a nobleman's daughter with elephantine feet. What an atrocious smell. Spray some lavender about and hand me a snip of rosewine. How can we afford to lose so many people?

FIRST MANDARIN.   The country, Ruler of all living things, is so thickly populated that a few human lives count for nothing. We can lose a million men without feeling the loss. [*Aside.*] This is really an insulting blend of obnoxious, desecrating stenches.

THE EMPEROR.   Give the poor devils something to eat. Deposit the rice right here. [FIRST MANDARIN *beckons to an attendant to carry out the order. During the following scene, rice is dumped down constantly in large quantities from the plateau.*] Who is that man over there?

FIRST MANDARIN.   Why that is Confucius! [*Aside.*] The brute, for whose sake we had to endure all the inconveniences of this trip through endless deserts of brown mud.

THE EMPEROR.   Why that shabby looking tramp! But look at the top of his head, like an urn. Carry me to him!

FIRST MANDARIN.   Did I hear right, O Genial Sun, carry you to him?

THE EMPEROR [*nods, the order is carried out*].   You are Confucius?

KUNG.   Yes.

[*The Villagers devour the raw rice with an expression of crazy stupor.*]

THE EMPEROR. Just stand over there and let me gaze at you. It pleases me just to feel your presence. You smell tolerably well.

KUNG. I do not perspire overmuch. Allow me to remain seated, I am rather weak in my legs.

FIRST MANDARIN. Seated in the presence of the Emperor. Why, he did not even join hands.

THE EMPEROR. Let be. —Why did you not accept the honor I wished to confer upon you? Why did you refuse to meet me?

KUNG. I do not know about that. If you had left matters to me, I would have probably made my appearance. As you commanded—I preferred to stay away. I am no bootlicker, I make and obey my own laws of conduct.

[CRAZY MOTHER *is heard drumming on the belly of her* CHILD.]

FIRST MANDARIN. What audacity! He deserves to be bastonnaded, O cloudless One.

THE EMPEROR. Let be. —I fail to comprehend. I am the Emperor.

KUNG. And I am Confucius.

THE EMPEROR [*frowning*]. You think you can rise to higher powers by letting the mob admire you?

KUNG. I do not care who admires me as long as I admire myself.

THE EMPEROR. You are spoilt. I have to be lenient with you.

KUNG. Not more so than with others. Don't get your dander up, Emperor. In this manner, we will not get along. What is the use of arguing. You cannot share my views. Nor I those of an Emperor. Should you care to speak to me any further, ask questions and I will answer them to my best knowledge and ability.

[*Rice is constantly dumped down from the Plateau. It covers the entire ground, and the* EMPEROR'S *retinue and* KUNG *have to continually lift their feet, as the surface of the rice rises higher and higher.*]

THE EMPEROR.   My subjects worship you as a sage; they call you the Son of a God.

KUNG.   Oh, the scribes of the Imperial Gazette—exaggerate, no doubt—I better move up a little so that this confounded quicksand of rice will not bury me. [*Rises.*]

THE EMPEROR.   What do you say to this?

KUNG.   In this world, it seems, all sorts of things may happen—creation is pain, and life is continuous creation. A more or less severe expression, what matters it.

THE EMPEROR.   I do not see why such things must happen. When I prayed daily in the temples for the welfare of my people, I did not realize that life could be so ugly and contain such pestilentious smells.

KUNG.   The Tiger's cubs can not be seen without going into his den.

THE EMPEROR.   Why do the gods permit it!

KUNG.   The gods, what do we know of them. Thousands of years men have bothered themselves about them, but they never revealed who they are, why they are, or that they are at all. If there are any gods, they apparently do not want us to know where they are; why should we bother about them.

[CRAZY MOTHER *is heard drumming on the belly of her* CHILD.]

THE EMPEROR [*meditating*].   True! [*Seizes* KUNG'S *little finger to poke the smoking weeds down into his pipe.*]

KUNG.   Kindly use your own finger.

FIRST MANDARIN.   O, Light unfathomable, the audacity of this man exceeds—

THE EMPEROR.   Let be. —What can I do for you, Kung? Autograph one of my portraits on silk for you?

KUNG.   Nothing in particular, ineffable one. Happiness

is supposed to be the aim of life, although too much of it makes one a laughing stock to the sad. Thus, I prefer to be passingly content.

THE EMPEROR. How do you manage it?

KUNG. By enjoying everything, even sorrow, sickness, every inconvenience, every irritation. Simply trying to struggle through to the vibrant golden sunshine in which nature is bathed at noon. If you suffer, try to enjoy it; look at it as a new adventure. There is something of interest even in the most disagreeable things. Hook on to it!

THE EMPEROR. I have, vulgarly speaking, griping pains down here. This scene has made me sick, I can get no enjoyment out of that.

KUNG. You may, as the pains pass away from you. But what is the use of explaining things that can be learned only by experience? Only in trivial acts man can be great.

THE EMPEROR. Then you have no special desires?

KUNG. None, except it were to stare as often as possible at a grey wall. The color pleases me. I also find a special relish in cutting my toenails, and ruminating about nothing while doing so.

[*Rice pours down in cataracts and fills the stage to half its height. The speakers move in jerks and jumps, finding it difficult to keep their legs above the surface.*]

THE EMPEROR. It must be frightfully monotonous, this doctrine of enjoying pain.

KUNG. Only few men are allowed to wear the yellow robe.

THE EMPEROR. I wish all my subjects were as content as you profess to be in all situations of life.

KUNG. You could do something towards it—and yet, I do not know. The golden middle way is a narrow line, so few can stay on it and reach the goal.

THE EMPEROR. What can I do? [KUNG *shrugs his shoulders.*] The world would not trust me. I know it as little as it

67

knows me. How can they trust me, when nobody is allowed to enter my palaces, when nobody has ever seen me eat, sleep, study, amuse myself, or watched me when I consider myself unobserved. I have never talked to a poor person, although I have realized during this journey that the majority of my subjects are poor. [*Attendants present a new coat; the* EMPEROR *continues to talk as he changes his dress.*] I have always been a patron of the arts. To tell the truth, I do not fancy playing the silkworm and shedding my robes so often. They sometimes make me wear fifty coats a day. As the same pattern can never be used again, I continually stimulate the artists to invent new designs.

KUNG.   Artists are not the only people living, although they seem to think so.

THE EMPEROR.   Do they not represent the ripest and best flavored fruit which falls from the tree of a nation?

KUNG.   Say rather soft-skinned hot-house fruit. We can get along without mushrooms as big as a starfish and camelias with treble chalices.

THE EMPEROR.   Confucius, I admire you. You, as you stand there, are a work of art, very queer and fascinating. What would you say if I cast aside my imperial robe, and descended from my throne. There shall be no more emperors. Like you, I will become an emperor among men.

KUNG.   Utterly absurd! Kindly stay on your throne if you entertain such sentiments. There is no use of making elaborate changes. Do the little you can. Tax the bachelors, for instance; and let the cares of tomorrow be borne by tomorrow.

THE EMPEROR.   I should at least show myself to the people.

KUNG.   What for! They would find out that you are as commonplace a person as all of us. Now you are, to fools at least, the Great Unseen.

FIRST MANDARIN.   This language, O peerless and impeccable one, exceeds—

THE EMPEROR.   You are right. They would consider me of wandering mind and somebody else would rule in my stead. You say, only few can reach the goal, I shall devote myself to them.

KUNG.   Ivory is found only in an elephant's mouth, and is in need of no improvement. You are too enthusiastic, Emperor.

THE EMPEROR.   Your indifference is also an extreme, Confucius.

KUNG.   The wisest of the two, perchance.

THE EMPEROR.   Possibly! Surely, something can be done.

KUNG.   No, Emperor, nothing can be done to set this world aright. I have tried my whole life to get myself into harmony with some part of the world, without much success, let others do the same. But what is the use of arguing!

[EMPEROR *spits into* KUNG'S *face.*]

KUNG.   Don't do that.

THE EMPEROR.   Does it annoy you? You galumphing sycophant!

KUNG.   Not in particular, you dream-struck sacrosanct! I am neither a horse nor of an amorous disposition. —A veritable snowstorm this! Riced in to the chest. You are an excellent stage manager, Emperor.

THE EMPEROR.   And you an exceptional actor, Confucius. After all, I have done more actual good than you. I have brought provisions, sufficient to last this community for a year.

KUNG.   There are not many left. The few that are still alive are demented and will die from overeating.

THE EMPEROR.   Then all this rice is wasted? Polished too, in my private grannaries.

KUNG.   The birds will feed on it—Emperor, you can not resist the material. It drowns everything, as I have re-marked repeatedly during our conversation, what is the use of arguing.

[*The heads of* KUNG, *the* EMPEROR *and his attendants disappear from sight. Rice fills the entire stage as the material element does our life.*]

KUNG. By the by, Emperor, I accept the position of Keeper of the Imperial Archives of Chow, provided you still care to give the job to me. Old men like their peanuts grated.

CURTAIN

ACT II

Scene IV. The Imperial Library of Chow

SCENE: *Interior of the Vaults containing the Imperial Archives of Chow. Several years later.*

KUNG [*enters in a robe of blue and grey, with piles of dusty parchments under his arms.*]. Now, I am the Keeper of the Imperial Archives of Chow, I wish I were on the Yellow River again. [*Blows dust from the parchments.*] The human soul enbalmed in these scriptures, how they would have spoken to me in former years, spoken of glorious inspiration, pleasure and joy, sadness and sorrow. Now they remain silent like pale visions that flit over desolate plains at night. [*Puts parchments aside.*]

Only one soul shines forth from the dim reminiscences of the past. The only one. And her shadow that once fell upon my life with fragrant calm, is clearer to me than the outlines of surrounding forms. Time separates us more and more, days are quick horsemen and change their horses often. I scarcely remember the sound of her voice. Men can live without everything on this earth, only not without domestic love. When fate has destroyed one illusion after the other, and the storms of autumn have defoliated leaf after leaf from the tree of life, only a loving soul like yours could warm a frostbitten soul like mine. [*Walks to the little golden shrine consecrated to the worship of his dead wife, and with trembling hands places roast fowl, fruit, wine and flowers before it, burns sweet smelling gums and lightens tapers of sandalwood and frankincense.*] The days I have spent with you on the

71

Yellow River live indestructibly in my soul; with unchangeable constancy the feeling of your worth and constancy remained in my heart—and for which I can find no other word, but affection. A friendship as it may seldom happen, a friendship that cannot be imagined less selfish and chaste, and yet a silent fanatic feeling of loyalty for you—of which death and so many years separate me.

Oh, that our roads could once more cross each other. I would glide to your feet and lean my face against your dress. You would see the wrinkles on my forehead, the hieroglyphics of experience, of sorrow and care, and you would tremble with sadness. To feel once more the currents of that sympathy, for more I do not ask—then our roads may separate again. Alas, it can not be! [*Takes a pinch of snuff.*]

What I have done, I had to do. I do not repent. I always worshipped you, although I could not always find expression for my reverence. I even failed to understand my own doctrine of domestic piety. I thought I was independent, rooted in myself, free from immediate influences. I thought my individuality was like a huge volcanic rock, that had risen by its inner force and loomed black of its own shadow austere over the sibilant seas, while dim sails, frail barks of other human thought, erred through the night like ghosts that can not find their graves.

I now realize that my life, my teachings, my individuality were sustained by your sympathy and love, that you were the creator of Confucius' thought as much as I. Life has burnt empty, a lamp without a wick. I have lost myself. Oh, that my head could rest once more on your lap, your warm breath caressing my forehead, while our baby's hand petted my cheek—that would be enough to fill eternity. [*In deep meditation begins to partake of the sacrificial food.*]

CURTAIN

The New Era of Mankind Begins to Sense Its Way

Buddha

A Drama in Twelve Scenes

(Written 1891-1895)

Persons Represented

GAUTAMA, *the Buddha*
LAGUDA ⎫
DAVKUNA ⎪
ZEANA ⎬ *bayaderes*
VAIVASVATA ⎭
PRINCE BERUSANI
NINDAR ⎫
SUDOTANA ⎭ *his tutors*
SENNA, *his attendant*
OLD MAN, *a dung collector*
A FATHER
FIRST PARIAH
SECOND PARIAH
JUGGLER
STUDENT
DEALER, *owner of a village store*
BLIND MAN
OLD MAN, *a lecher*
WOMAN, *whose lover has left*
YOUNG GIRL
FIRST STEWARD ⎫
SECOND STEWARD ⎬ *retainers of the Naked King*
THIRD STEWARD ⎭
NAKED KING
NOBLEMAN
NURVA, *the Magi of Odors*
YOUNG BARBARIAN CHIEFTAIN
ARIYA, *a crippled maiden*

THE WISE OLD MAN
OLD VILLAGER
FIRST MAIDEN ⎫
SECOND MAIDEN ⎬ *the maidens draped in lilac*
THIRD MAIDEN ⎭
FIRST DISCIPLE ⎫
SECOND DISCIPLE ⎪
THIRD DISCIPLE ⎬ *the five Holy Disciples of Buddha*
FOURTH DISCIPLE ⎪
FIFTH DISCIPLE ⎭

Inhabitants of the Villages, Priests, Worshippers, Nuns, Monks, Double Choir, Child Riding Lion, Pilgrims, Barbarians, Female Captives, etc.

Synopsis

TIME: About 500 B.C.

SCENE I

Shore of Drifting Sand. View on the Ocean Moondawn

SCENE: *Gautama asleep on the dunes. A train of camels approaches. The former silence seems to be heightened by the cautious, gliding, indolent steps of the camels, to which the waves murmur a faint accompaniment.*

GAUTAMA [*awakes, and gazes motionless, as if still dreaming, on the silent procession—ghost-like as their flitting shadows— until the last camel has disappeared in the greenish distance*]. As human life should be! Art's fragrance wafted by, that in orgasmic joys incessantly dissolves life's ambiguity.

CURTAIN

SCENE II

On the Banks of the Ganges

SCENE: *To the left, through a rich confusion of white and scarlet rhododendron trees, interspersed with luxuriant tropical growth, silvery glimpses of the river; in the center a hill, over which a reddish road ascends from the right. Drowsy, vibrating light of noontide. Now and then, a sluggish draught moves gently through the scene, and the trees shake dreamingly their leafy crowns.*

BAYADERES: LAGUDA, DAVKUNA, ZEANA *and* VAIVASVA-TA *enter; their golden girdles glitter as they make their way through the jungles.*

LAGUDA.   A day bewildering and fervent sweet!

DAVKUNA.   The sun progresses to his height of passion; all flowers fade beneath his violence.

ZEANA.   Not a snake or lizard sparkles in the ferns and moss.

DAVKUNA.   No incantation of an iridescent bird is sounding.

ZEANA.   The gnats alone perform their tremulous dance.

DAVKUNA.   The water beckons with fragrant calm.

VAIVASVATA.   Why do you undrape so hastily?

LAGUDA.   To come in contact with nature. It is as if the dust of daily toil were falling from my body, and I became a better and purer being when naked.

VAIVASVATA.   I like to unsheathe myself, slowly, softly, one by one, with long intervals. [*Breaks a flower and looks*

79

into its chalice, lost in contemplation; butterflies of every conceivable hue flutter around her.]

LAGUDA [*throwing off her last garment*]. No, I must drink in nature, like a thirsty babe its mother's milk; inhale light and air with every sense, feel at once the water's full embrace and allow its resilient waves to caress and kiss me without truce—without rest—without end. [*Runs off.*]

DAVKUNA [*looking after her*]. What a streak of light!

ZEANA. Brightest bit of color imaginable! The despair of painters.

DAVKUNA. Laguda has unfastened her auburn hair. Now, she will duck. Look—a nymph disappearing in the waves of her own dishevelled hair!

VAIVASVATA [*to the flower*]. Like a sister soul whose rhythmic breath of unavowed desires deflowers all the pregnant sounds of passion!

[PRINCE BERUSANI, *his tutors* NINDAR *and* SUDOTANA, *and* SENNA, *an attendant, appear on the highway.*]

PRINCE BERUSANI. Is this their trysting place?

SENNA. Like moving statues they nudate. Transparent clouds pass softly over heaven.

NINDAR. Then shade your eyes, for you will be mad with desire; a sunray struggling golden through the grey of clouds seems more triumphant than the sun of love itself.

PRINCE BERUSANI. Wherefore restraint upon restraint? All animals delight in mutual fellowship—the plants sway to and fro each other, even the rocks bend towards the sun and heave their granite souls up to the moon—why should not men and women consecrate their spring by love!

SUDOTANA. Because it merges man in countless troubles and vexations.

ZEANA. There is no doubt that we are the four most roseate rorulent love maidens in the district.

DAVKUNA [*to* ZEANA]. Chaste furies of diurnal storms have carved thy tapering limbs.

ZEANA. Vaivasvata is beauty's queen.

VAIVASVATA. My body is too luxuriant, deep and cold.

ZEANA [*to* VAIVASVATA]. In warlike hemispheres thy body's soul reveals itself.

DAVKUNA. Then her abdomen, long and bold, melodious warm, and chastely vaulted! In ruined rhythms flow the lines of mine.

VAIVASVATA. And lies the garden of thy love forlorn!

ZEANA. Who carves in ivory the ardent silver of her lily breasts?

DAVKUNA. Upon whom, I wonder, would Prince Berusani bestow his flaming kiss?

ZEANA. Beauty blurs by dew of love and sighs of passion. [*picks up a handful of broken petals.*] Behold, can thy languid eyes discern which one was blown by winds of night, on seas of love between thy pleasure lips?

VAIVASVATA [*sits as if thinking of past experiences of love*]. Scented winds blow gently, kiss my nakedness and scatter flower leaves and pollen dust upon my trembling self.

DAVKUNA [*rests herself on a rock*]. I like to sit on hot stones, and full of devotion adore the beautiful, odorous summer day. It intoxicates me like Soma wine. [*Smiling; her lustrous eyes half closed.*]

ZEANA [*laughs*]. What queer little waves tumble over the pebbles and pet my soles. This is heavenly! The lapping of the waves, the distant noises on the highway, the whispering of the tree-tops! The birth of slumbering varicolored songs!

[DAVKUNA *staggers into the water.*]

VAIVASVATA [*naked*]. What harmony of lambent sounds each movement of the body lilts! Ah, to sing and dance the raptures of love in this realm of light! [*Makes a few dignified steps while humming a festive air.*] Proudly I step into the cool and tempting flood. What a beautiful reflection I make in the water!

PRINCE BERUSANI.   The water purls from her limbs as from the shining petals of the water lily without leaving trace. For her I could put my hands into a furnace.

NINDAR.   Believe me, oh Prince, each urn of love is filled with filth or poison. These women are like fruit before its fall: luscious and over-ripe. Behold them lolling with themselves at night, engulfed in twilight blanks of ruined flowers, fallen gems, and finery unthrilled by lute and tambourine; you'll awake from your dream and, in the nauseous atmosphere of amorous vulgarity, see womankind deprived of her fictitious love-breath charms. One has earth-drawn breasts that no babe can suckle; another suggests in wrinkles the vapidness of fat senility; a third one's face reveals in sleep the ugliness of her soul.

PRINCE BERUSANI.   Is it always the body which we love?

SENNA.   No woman will refuse you the enjoyment of her soul. Yet taste her body first to test whether your love be really searching for her soul.

PRINCE BERUSANI.   Well spoken, Senna; let these buddhas talk; we two shall act.

SUDOTANA.   Though men know that to enjoy woman means distress, they are ever impatient for new follies for their sake.

PRINCE BERUSANI.   Now they shake liquid pearls from hair and limb. Let us sweep down like lovelorn winds on high-stalked flowers and search for bliss in dim treasure caves amidst liquescent wilderness! [*Tearing the obstructing branches apart.*]

GAUTAMA [*appears; murmurs in a monotonous, long-drawn, hypnotizing voice, repeating every sentence three times, as he slowly passes on*].   Renounce! Humanity, renounce all confident conviction in yourself! Struggle for the cessation of sorrow, become ensouled in me; the Sublime Renunciation, The Non-God. [*Exits.*]

[SENNA *stares enquiringly at* PRINCE BERUSANI, *who gazes*

motionless after GAUTAMA. NINDAR *and* SUDOTANA *stand in ecstasy, hushed by the mystery of soul concussion. The Bayaderes, exhaling tremulous diffidence and broken indecision, have seized some of their garments and hide behind foliage, only* VAIVASVATA *looms up radiant in triumphant monotony.*]

CURTAIN

SCENE III

A Village Street

SCENE: *Change of scene to a village street produced by moving scenery.* PRINCE BERUSANI, *followed by* NINDAR *and* SUDO-TANA, *whose faces show the dull, stereotype smile of Indian statues, walk along the street.*

OLD MAN [*collecting dry dung*]. Alas—alas—alas!

BERUSANI. Why do you sigh so pitifully?

OLD MAN. Pick up dung yourself, and you will know why.

BERUSANI. Imagine that it is an agreeable and renumerative occupation.

OLD MAN. Are you one of those poets who make gold of camel's dung? I have no use for them. Don't babble any more. I won't understand your parables. [*Continues his work.*] Alas—alas—alas!

BERUSANI. How stupid to live in these little houses, when one can have the whole universe as abode. Human beings are the queerest things in creation.

[*A FATHER stands at the threshold of a cottage. A beautiful mother fondles her child.*]

BERUSANI [*steps up to them*]. Do not be too happy; calamities may come at any moment. Your husband may play false, or your sudden death may leave the child to strangers.

FATHER. Go along, you philosophizing mendicants. Don't frighten a little woman, or I'll try my fist on your shaven crowns.

[*Two* PARIAHS *with cramped limbs and swollen bellies crawl through the dust.*]

FIRST PARIAH. Pray, give me more than you can spare!

SECOND PARIAH. Don't be cluntch-fisted. Offer a sacrifice to poverty, personified in me!

BERUSANI. We have less than you. You see we are satisfied and do not make such faces.

FIRST PARIAH. You are healthy, while we—ah me, what pain!

BERUSANI. Console yourselves; we wear a girdle of thorns around our waists. [*Shows his thighs, on which blood drops are visible.*]

SECOND PARIAH. They are mad. Ah me—what pain!

[JUGGLER *showing his tricks to the crowd.*]

BERUSANI. You are the symbol of humanity! —Juggling, juggling, always juggling; trying to stand on your heads for no earthly reason whatever; dancing on ropes and listening to soothsaying.

JUGGLER. Get out of the way, and don't spoil honest people's business.

[*In the next cottage a* STUDENT *is seen writing.*]

HIS FATHER [*proudly*]. Look out for him; some day he will be a great buddha.

BERUSANI. Do not cudgel your brain, poor fool, your mental gravity will cause neither revolution nor enlightment. I fear you cannot even comprehend that, alone, the mind which—were it but for one short hour—reigned ubiquitous in other souls, still conscious of itself, could discard the partiality of self and gain omniscience among man. Poor drudge!

STUDENT. Ruffian, you dare! I forget myself. Seers who describe the indescribable should suffer martyrdom in indestructible passivity.

[DEALER *counts his money in a little store.*]

BERUSANI. If you lay aside as much as that each day, you will soon be a worthy partisan of wealth.

DEALER [*chuckles*].   Yes, I have laid by a goodly sum.

BERUSANI.   Some night robbers might break into your house and kill you; of what use would your coins then be to you except to be smelted into an urn for your ashes?

DEALER [*raking up his money*].   Help! Thieves, robbers!

BLIND MAN [*passes by*].   Have pity with the blind man! Tell me where I am.

BERUSANI.   Dear friend, none of us knows where he is. Men do not even know where this world is floating in the universe.

BLIND MAN.   What are you mumbling about? Do you take me for a fool? Can I not hear, taste, smell, feel what others see?

[*An* OLD MAN, *toothless, trembling upon his stick, leers at a young girl, who walks with an affected, rocking gate.*]

BERUSANI.   Are you not ashamed of yourself, old, dissipated wretch?

OLD MAN [*grins, pointing after the girl*].   At the first glance I espy the most hidden lines.

BERUSANI.   Are you not old enough to know that the lusts of man are like sea water, mocking man's thirst instead of quenching it?

[OLD MAN *grins; leaning forward on his stick, he falls down.*]

WOMAN [*beats her breast, tears her hair, and casts away her jewels*].   Woe is me! Woe is me!

BERUSANI.   What woe has befallen you?

WOMAN.   My lover has left me.

BERUSANI.   Weep, as the years gyrate, or search for other currents consanguineous in love to yours.

[NINDAR *and* SUDOTANA *stop spellbound for a moment at the sight of a barber shaving the head of a child.* NINDAR *stares at the bald head of the child,* SUDOTANA *at the razor glistening in the sun; thereupon both pursue their way, their faces having completely changed expression and become illumined as if by a new idea. A corpse lying on a bier is carried out of the village; lamenting women follow it.*]

BERUSANI.   Why do you whine, as if you were losing your wits, over one who is no more, or attained a state of future bliss? Why do you not dance and sing, and feast? They hate death, and yet wish to be reborn in another world! [*Leaving the village they encounter a young girl.*] What are you searching for in the grass?

YOUNG GIRL.   For flowers hitherto unknown.

[NINDAR *and* SUDOTANA *for the first time nod approval. In the distance looms a row of gigantic pagodas.*]

NINDAR.   Fare thee well, oh Prince. Here our ways do part.

SUDOTANA.   Never to meet again, I hope.

NINDAR and SUDOTANA.   You wend your way from whence we came.

BERUSANI.   And whither will your future lead?

NINDAR and SUDOTANA.   To flowers hitherto unknown. [*Exit.*]

BERUSANI.   Must I fain meander through this labyrinthian life alone!

CURTAIN

The Temple of Renunciation

SCENE: *Court corner in a cave temple (as Menzel might paint it), with shrines, images and basins for holy water. Crowds of worshippers; some turn praying wheels. Bell-ringing. Somber atmosphere. A Double Choir performs the majestic hymn of painful exuberance: "Let good will without measure prevail among beings. Even in this world holiness may be found."*
LAGUDA, DAVKUNA, ZEANA *and* VAIVASVATA, *robed in opal and celadon, listen.*

LAGUDA.   Like surging waves these mighty rhythms rush upon me!

ZEANA.   As a high-stalked flower trembles in the wind, listlessly I sway hither and thither under the currents of these fierce and pregnant melodies. I fain will die, if not a simpler chord, on which my life is set, sounds forth. [*Listens as if time and space were gone.*]

DAVKUNA [*like a back-blown, dew-pearled flower*]. Meseems that lilies sprout upon lutescent hills and in the deepest depths of forest-wilds. Oh, fleeting moments of voluptuous pain!

VAIVASVATA.   Oh, knights of heaven, come, redeem me from the throes of continence, squandering our energy to act like men.

[*The singing ceases. Three* STEWARDS, *though dressed like princes, converse steward-like to* GAUTAMA, *leaning against a colossal Bangalore. A magnificent procession passes by: incense*

*and flower bearers, shaven priests in gorgeous vestments, monks
and nuns of the Huge Convent, with fans, lamps, sacred vessels,
etc., etc.*]

SECOND STEWARD.   All is over now.

THIRD STEWARD.   He has really squandered his kingdom. Who would have believed it?

FIRST STEWARD.   And what a festival it was!

THIRD STEWARD.   Since its beginning, darkness devoured the moon some twenty times.

SECOND STEWARD [*to* GAUTAMA].   It would have probably changed your system of meditation, you old hypocrite.
Fifty kings from shore and mountain-land and the vast
plains attended; none as magnanimous as he.

THIRD STEWARD.   They came in four-horsed chariots of
gold and precious stones; the parade of their retinue often
lasted six hours.

FIRST STEWARD.   One procession of white elephants was
one mile long. You never heard such trumpeting before.

SECOND STEWARD.   And the horse sacrifice! By all that is
glorious!

THIRD STEWARD.   More splendid pavilions of pleasure
never were pitched upon the banks of the Ganges.

FIRST STEWARD.   The woods were swarming with bayaderes.

THIRD STEWARD.   Music was performed night and day
by thousands of instruments.

SECOND STEWARD.   And the twelve-act dramas; what
moral edification!

THIRD STEWARD.   Lights, flickering in every hue imaginable, flashed through the forests, and from the mountain
peaks, through all dark hours.

FIRST STEWARD.   And now he is adored by his people.
Larger multitudes, men and women, old and young, poor
and sick, never feasted together.

THIRD STEWARD.   All the gods were regilded.

SECOND STEWARD. Everybody's portrait was painted gratuitously.

THIRD STEWARD [to GAUTAMA]. Well may astonishment render you silent. Such a miracle of benevolence was unknown before.

SECOND STEWARD. He is too good for this world. He wished to apply the laws of heaven to ungrateful humanity. Should he ever repent of having squandered everything, he may take my possessions—and yours too, eh!

FIRST STEWARD. Yes, I give in. He was very kind to us.

THIRD STEWARD. As it was he who presented me with those thickly manured fields, my future home enclosed by shady trees, he may sit under them and bouse from the cistern whenever he likes.

SECOND STEWARD [to GAUTAMA]. You would like to know why he did it. He felt a yearning which nothing could satisfy and which robbed all charm from earthy glories and hopes.

FIRST STEWARD. He does not seem interested.

THIRD STEWARD. Do not bother about that fool.

FIRST STEWARD. He must be a little weak-minded.

SECOND STEWARD. The king is coming! Naked! He has given away his last robe. Let us weep over his generosity.

[The KING enters.]

ALL EXCEPT GAUTAMA. We bow before thee, holy man! We praise thy wisdom's adamantine glory, which gropes in the dark confusion of this world for wisdom's piercing light.

[A female child, decorated with jewels and holding a mirror, riding on a lion, is led by.]

NAKED KING. Behold this child with the pearl and ruby-rimmed mirror: egotism reflecting truth. Just as the mirror relates to our eyes the occurrences of the surrounding scene, so does the image-forming soul of children dimly reflect the outside world, of which involuntarily they regard themselves the center. The circle of vision widens as they grow older; less than ever can they escape from this delusion. We grown-up children, in our self-importance, spend the largest part of our existence in selfish desire and care, longing for objects unattainable which, when attained, produce no happiness, but fresh desire and care. Therefore, it is wisest to reduce our wants to naught. As a king, as the great I am, I could easily follow my heart's desire without transgressing right, let me try if I can also live in bane on the common ways of life.

GAUTAMA [*remaining in his earth-lorn attitude.*]. Renounce! Humanity, renounce all confident conviction in yourself! Struggle for the cessation of sorrow, and become ensouled in me, the Sublime Renunciation, the Non-God!

[NAKED KING *makes a stupid face.*]

[*Fluid silver threads fall slanting from the bowels of the universe, and lightnings tear a fringe of vibrate fire-gold athwart the darkened robe of heaven.*]

CURTAIN

SCENE V

The Lake of Individual Aristocracy

SCENE: *Sad silence over a lake lost in the solitude of a nobleman's park. Cranes stand amidst high-stalked flowers on the edge of the crystalline water. Swans float dream-like among the white, red and blue lotuses, who, trembling in odorous satiety, lift their immaculate chalices into the musical atmosphere.*

NOBLEMAN [*robed in virgated violescence, with a dazed and absorbed look, rests in a giant tortoise shell filled with Madhavi blossoms, extending hospitality to the two pilgrims,* NINDAR *and* SUDOTANA, *sitting cross-legged. They have paper stripes with Yama, the god of death, fastened to their hempen robes.* NINDAR *hides a dagger on his hairy chest. Slaves fan them*].   So you have met the genuine Buddha? [*Pilgrims nod.*] And he had such an overwhelming influence upon you, for after all it was he who induced you to change your lives completely. He must exercise a strange hypnotizing influence, that old—how should I name him? I also admired him in former times when his irresistible eloquence made crowds of thousands stand motionless. Nevertheless, I was always of the opinion that he tried to make rather too much of himself. You know he had the trick of carrying blue lights about his person, in a manner as if he himself radiated the light. As for his conceit in letting the sages of the country dispute whether his mother bore him in a horizontal or vertical position—pshaw! He has also proclaimed that he is

god himself. All this, of course, is absurd. Nevertheless, he
will be one of the greatest thinkers of all time; perhaps, who
can vouch for it, the founder of hundreds of religions. Every
millennium a wise man is born who, with words of truth,
strews sand into the brains of all; and they, who anyhow
have no time or ability to think, perch parrot-like about,
roting his words. Peculiar are your two theories. You
[*Turning to* SUDOTANA.], to kill all, especially the viable, and
throw their corpses into the river by night, so that sailors of
the ocean may gaze on them, gnawed by vultures, floating
with bloated bellies [*Makes a movement of disgust.*] away into
the dim unknown. And you [*to* NINDAR.], to teach mankind
to avoid the nuptial state, thus calling forth the dissolution
of the race. You two work hand in hand. If you succeed in
preventing birth, and you kill off the living, the world will
soon whirl depopulated through the universe. I understand
you: you have grown weary of life. As for me, possessing
various talents—I sing, write poetry, paint and sculpt a
little—I should find life tolerable at least. I can lie for hours
and listen to pearls pattering over marble slabs, or to the
crackling of silk under old wenches' horny finger-ends. And
what delight, to have my languid limbs deluged with oils
and wines, each fluid, like each paramour, caressing me in
different grades of bliss. Yet, one man, after all, can accomplish so little, even if he ravished earth's nations with
ardent swords, or conjured up towers of Babel with despo-
tism's bloody fist. What can we really know! They say the
world is an immense ball, circling through space, I believe. I
am no astronomer—I must believe in hearsay. Therefore, I
have perfect right to imagine it an eclipse or a pyramid. And
as far as human experience in sorrow is concerned—how
insignificant! We cannot even realize what we have experienced. Only the great fireworker may express uncon-
sciously the melancholy of a thousand lives with one fire
line piercing the nocturnal sky. I also feel weary at times,

for I have acquired neither great wisdom nor keen power of reasoning. I possess but delitescent intuition; and it teaches me that he is best off who, like the butterfly, injuring not the color or scent of his beloved flowerlets, flies away after sipping the nectar. So I sing, write poetry, paint and sculpt a little. And in regard to joy in living, I can assert without conceit, that I have acquired one rather high-strung preference: I do not receive the same impression of things as other men do; they always consider my impression false, peculiar, vague, or exaggerated; and I feel that, after all—my taste for after-flavors seems superior—is, perhaps, the only true one— [*pilgrims shake their heads*] that is the only true one to me—to none else—beautiful, good, sacred *is* what I experience so! However, let us have some recreation. [*Beckons.*]

[NURVA, *the Magi of Odors, dressed in jewels and a veil of black transparency, appears. In her left arm rests a lyre in ivory and gold. She assumes a hieratic attitude, with her right arm makes a mysterious, sweeping gesture through the languid atmosphere, and strikes a few harmonious accords on her instrument. A delicate scent is wafted from her, which changes whenever her right hand repeats the mystic sign and falls like fugitive kisses on the trembling chords. Her performance reveals the psychological wealth of odors, the possibilities of an olfactory art. The melodious colors of perfume subdue the illusion of reality; and the mind, laden with scent, soars into unknown realms of imagination, where desire alone is law. And in everchanging symphonies the odors suggest all sensation and embrace eternity. In the beginning the Magi suggests in intermingling harmonies the laughter of youth o'er green velvety meadowland, the flowers of subtlest emotions exhaling once more the dividuous scents of their violated chalices to the fading sun, or aromatic balms (of vegetable substances) suggesting the silent reveries of night: when human lights extinguish and the moon, pale as if woven by fairy tales, mourns over dark cypress trees; then paraphrasing on the sweat of labor, the sea of*

*multi-odorous life surges by in bold impressionistic dreams,
strewn with the rafters of despair in variations of ambergris
resembling the colors of Chavannes, ebbing at last on solitary
strains of ardent unadulterated smells into timeless meditations
over the Nothing, boring deep holes into consciousness—stark
still pauses on the wisdom of renunciation—like the acrid,
passionless litany of lilies.*]

[*During this scene* NINDAR *has repeatedly scratched himself
and plucked his nose; and* SUDOTANA *has nervously groped for
his dagger; he now jumps up and stabs the nobleman.*]

NOBLEMAN [*falling out of the shell*]. Is this the way you
repay hospitality?

NINDAR. What have you done?

SUDOTANA. Began the mission of my life! [*Stabbing at the
attendants who try to seize him; to* NINDAR.] You I allow to
live; you are my ally in this work! [*Escapes.*]

NOBLEMAN. Let me try at least to die in as comfortable
and picturesque a manner as circumstances allow. [*Holding
some perfume to his nose and with the other hand pressing his
wound, assumes a theatrical pose.*] Inform my guests, that I
beg to be excused, as I am engaged in dying.

[*The startled cranes wing away in lyric lines from the
high-stalked flowers, sighing beneath the melancholy incanta-
tions of the wind; the lotuses drown their chalices in the languid
undulations of their watery bed; while the swans, shivering,
assemble and, in mystic attitudes, fade away into the darkness.*]

CURTAIN

SCENE VI

A Battlefield

SCENE: *Sunset changing into cold russet. Long-haired and long-limbed barbarians in leopard skins rob the corpses, lying in every position, distorted and bleeding, of all ornaments of value. Female captives crouch in fear and shame in agonistic outlines against the passive sky. Rows of elephants in the distance.*

YOUNG BARBARIAN CHIEFTAIN [*in a gorgeous dress, over-loaded with sparkling jewels, and smeared with blood; one foot in the cleft skull of his father*].   Like a hissing tide of fire, we coiled devouring through the hostile lines with many a crackling blaze, until they self-oblivious fled, and my infuriated herd of elephants, with spearing tusk and crushing trunk, surged after them and tread the cowards down in murderous rage. Here I have fought my greatest victory! Yet I feel sad, since I have seen that white emaciated loafer—it must have been a buddha. I did not understand the meaning of his murmurings; to me it meant: Why are you raving of immortal glory, if your tomorrow dawns perchance on fate more cruel than your foes' tonight? Why the incessant relentless strife with this old fool? [*Pushes aside the skull with his toes.*] Like youth, I faced the East, garnered my strength from dawn's invigorance; while your red eyes, white bearded man, sought constantly the panorama of the setting sun which blinded you to life's realities. We two, like all, looked upon different worlds, although we stood so close together. A disgust has come over me. I dislike the sharp, bright edge of my barbaric sword. Spoliation, rape and slaughter were my religion hitherto, and with one stroke to split in two a human body its orgasmic height. Perhaps it was my liking living red; now I want white—the white of human bodies without wounds and scars—and crack from my hands the gore of weeks. [*Muses.* THE NAKED KING, *ornamented with flowers, passes.*] And thou, strange wanderer, I would heap upon thee all the spoils of this year's bordraging, if thou wert not a thousa d times more beautiful in the wholeness of thy flawless mould. Oh, could we all live flower-crowned, in sexless beauty, in marble homes, amidst dark foliage, 'neath azure skies!

THE NAKED KING [*pursuing his meandering*]. Why hope, date after date, expecting a better day by some change alway; if, at any rate, whatever we try to do will end with the same old fate!

[*The infamies of war are fading in the crepuscular mist; here and there the jewels on some corpses gleam in the gore of the vanished sun.*]

CURTAIN

SCENE VII

At the Forest Edge of Life

SCENE: *To the left an old, dilapidated tent pitched up at the forest edge which, winding itself into the distance, forms a slanting line across the background; between the latter and the foreground a sloping plain. To the right, at the edge of an abyss, a solitary fir tree, from where a wide vista on the surrounding country can be enjoyed. Early evening effect.*

ARIYA [*a lean, ugly, crippled maid at the age of opening buds—her eyes radiate an almost unearthly inward beauty— balancing on her head a large dish with red rice dumplings and carrying a jug filled with curdled milk on her hip, enters, looks about and listens*].   The winds of eventide stray through the forest. The wings of insects sing to nubile buds, husks yield and stamens expand in dewlit depths.

THE WISE OLD MAN [*is seen rolling down the sloping plain towards his tent; as he rises he bursts out into an Aristophanic roar of laughter which shakes his whole frame*].   How life is interesting! Ah, Ariya! Why, what saturity; heavy to carry, eh? The nuns of the Huge Convent must really consider me a glutton. There was a time when I could easily manage this in one sitting, but those days of voracity are over; now a dish of rice with a fragrant sauce—I am getting incanescent, Ariya. When I awake in the morning [*draws* ARIYA *on his knees*] I am perfectly stiff. I can't move my joints. They get out of place during the night. I begin to rub, beat, scrape myself all over with a piece of rhinoceros skin, and gradu- ally I am able to stretch, bend, use my limbs. After dragging about for awhile, cheered, strengthened, I feel more comfortable, and by vespertime I am lively enough to afford myself the pleasure of rolling, sliding, tumbling down this hill. [*Lets* ARIYA *glide from his knee and toddles to the solitary fir tree.*] Oh, you sly rascal, up to your tricks again!

ARIYA. I wonder how you can do it without growing dizzy.

WISE OLD MAN. I have balanced myself long enough over the inconsistent absurdities of life, and I can now well afford to stand firmly at this precipice and . . . . . . this foolish, foolish world.

ARIYA. Interfered with by nobody? How enviable!

WISE OLD MAN. If human beings want to live peacefully they should even beware of friends—grow indurate.

ARIYA. I, then, do not want to be your friend—

WISE OLD MAN. Never so profane a thing. I love you as I love the rocks, the trees, the atmosphere.

ARIYA. For I have only you to go to. Nobody likes me.

WISE OLD MAN. They are your saintly eyes they do not like. They arouse suspicion.

ARIYA. Do you never feel lonesome?

WISE OLD MAN. Lonesome with myself as company? On the contrary, sometimes—to my own humiliation, I confess this stain on my content—I struggle to get away, sneak out from my personality, as everything seems so amusing, so ridiculous to me. I have such fits of laughter that tears gush over my cheeks and I finally fall asleep exhausted. My cup of life is full, overflowing, inexhaustible. The world lies before me like a stage, with a mystery play upon the programme. I espy princely hunts and crowded fairs, religious processions and marching armies, enough to suggest the insoluble problems of existence without being annoyed by its trivialities. From time to time the curtain drops, wrapping me in a cloud of mist, whereupon nature begins anew to tease and tickle me with her inconsequent monstrosities. If it be not a sumptuous psalm of sunset, a drowsy noonday lullaby of heat, or the furious rhythms of a thunderstorm, an inundation or an earthquake may be served to me as an irresistible side-splitting delicacy. What flaring lights pierce through the forest? It reminds me of yesternight. Do you see yonder smoking ruins? A burning village furnished fireworks for me.

[*An infuriated and lamenting crowd of villagers drag in* SUDOTANA *by his legs, his head trailing on the ground.*]

BAWLING OF THE MOB. Justice! Hail to thee, perpetual laughter! We found a dead monkey in our well. We anticipated a croak disaster. It has come. This monster set our village on fire. He is a massacrist. He has robbed us. He has killed us. We, all you see here, are almost dead.

WISE OLD MAN [*grins*]. A tragical farce, Ariya. Do not reflect it in tears, my child. The mob is not worthy of such dew.

ARIYA. I feel people's sorrow by the music they exhale.

OLD VILLAGER. They wanted to lynch him—

CROAKING OF THE MOB. Starve him to death! —Skin him alive! —Nail him to a tree! —Cut him in two! —No, cut him in 120 pieces! —At least defer the cuts affecting vital organs to the last!

WISE OLD MAN. Murderer's murderers!

OLD VILLAGER. I, putting my own life in danger, protected him, as we have to be just even to monstrosities. Let us go to the Wise Old Man, I advised, and let him sit judgment on this infandous crime.

WISE OLD MAN. How his gaping wounds encrimson the ground!

OLD VILLAGER. Gaze at this woman. [*Pointing at a woman who holds a singed body in her arms.*] Was it your only child?

WOMAN. Oh, no; if it had been, it would have just killed me. I have lost other children before, but never one like this.

[*Kisses the singed body.*] I never knew what death meant.

OLD VILLAGER.   Oh, what pain has been suffered on this earth! Why are we created to endure such tortures, which will in twilight hours still reverberate when the sufferers are long dead.

WISE OLD MAN.   Why so yond, old yowler?

OLD VILLAGER.   Gaze at this old man. [*An old man, stiff as a log of wood, is carried by two villagers to the foreground.*] He was the hoariest man in our village. He had just hundred and seventeen children and grandchildren; one three-legged absurdity among them. They are all burnt; their bodies char under yonder ruins! When he saw his house sway creaking and groaning from side to side, and finally tumble over burying domestic happiness and wealth under a cloud of dust, he seemed to lose all life and stands like a statue ever since.

WISE OLD MAN.   You seem to take relish in such things, old scape-cross?

SUDOTANA.   I am their misjudged benefactor. They should rejoice that I endeavor to shorten their disgusting slavery to nature and each other, instead of maltreating him who despises life.

WISE OLD MAN.   Not so much as to annihilate yourself, eh, old scape-cross?

SUDOTANA.   I am doomed to preserve my detestable life; I have still other deeds to do.

WISE OLD MAN.   Egregious! Set him free. He is a superior being: he has a conviction. Don't throp, dear folks, go home without verbosity; you have not lost much, as you never owned, appropriated, adopted a conviction. Profit by this zealot incarnation—acquire one.

CRUNCHING OF THE MOB.   Shame! Shame! Is this rectitude? —That is beyond me. —At least let him pay a fine. —Why has he the right to commit such an outrage?

WISE OLD MAN.   Because he is more powerful than you.

101

Justice is an empty word; whether he be right or wrong, only one judge can decide: he himself. Whatever you have the power to be, you have the right to do.

BARKING OF THE MOB. Is that so? —Ahem! —You enlighten us! —Let us try? etc.

[*An enamoured young villager springs panther-like upon the wife of another villager, who enraged stabs him in the back, so that the entangled couple rolls into the abyss.*]

WISE OLD MAN. Quab-disciple!

SNARLING OF THE MOB [*as they disperse*]. Next time we'll go to the Wise Old Woman who always weeps. I am weary of his umpireship. He is fast getting decrepit; wisdom is passing out of his reach.

WISE OLD MAN. Come, Ariya, let us repose in our flesh.

ARIYA [*to* SUDOTANA]. What can we do for you?

SUDOTANA. Untie my ropes.

WISE OLD MAN. Unnecessary labor! You would fall to pieces.

ARIYA. Why, you are badly hurt.

WISE OLD MAN. Not much left; quite unfleshed.

SUDOTANA [*struggles to rise*]. I must go to work. There are still so many living.

[GAUTAMA *passes along the forest edge in the distance; his white garment is seen flitting through the tree trunks.* SUDO-TANA *sinks down, staring at the apparition.*]

WISE OLD MAN. Won't you try and take a good dinner, and thereupon let me kick you into the abyss. No? You want to die right here on the spot? [*Scratching his head.*] But, dear friend, imagine what outrageous, pestiferous smells you'll make. We have such scorching nights at this time of the year. Well, as you like, suit yourself. Come, Ariya. [*Sits down before the tent to eat his supper, suddenly bursts out into a roar of laughter.*] How life is interesting!

CURTAIN

102

SCENE VIII

The Valley of Rest

SCENE: *A road lined with cypress trees descends through a landscape of superb breadth and beauty, towards one of the colossal, highly fantastical palaces of India, lit up with a few soft lights. Early evening effect, varying from a faint lilac green to a deep violet.*

GAUTAMA [*enters*].   The world with its tumults lies behind me. The battlefields and fighting hosts of yesterday are but indistinct masses in agitated lines. Onwards and onwards I move to unknown heights. Before I pursue my path, let me rest a few moments in this valley of peace. All here breathes quietude and plentitude, serenity without alloy, untainted with burdening thoughts and woes of transitoriness. My home, my home! In all my errantry for these scores of years, I never found a place so spellfull, seductive, so radiant with bliss, such holy calm as this. The sweet, pure delights of home and love, the charm of wealth and power, glow once more in their alluring lights. They are within my reach. I would be welcomed back, and yet—how could they give me satisfaction now?

[THREE MAIDENS *draped in lilac with severe simplicity, seem to float through the still evening air.* GAUTAMA *stands as if petrified.*]

FIRST MAIDEN.   As we wander homewards, tell me once more the story of the cruel, holy man.

THIRD MAIDEN. I think of it by day and dream of it by night.

SECOND MAIDEN. Listen, then: —It had been a summer day like this, fifty years gone by. The evening was a lovely dream-hipped maiden like yourself; deepening space was like her flowing robes; the dark clouds like her braided hair; the stars like precious stones adorning beauty. And the Prince, the pride of India, whispered gently: "Yasodhara, dear wife, it is late. Go to rest." She answered with shimmering tears in the chalice of her lotus eyes: "I am alarmed at your sadness of late, oh Prince, my soul of all." He fondled her lovingly, kissing her moist bimba lips: "Let not such anxieties cause you distress." So she went musing to her jasmine-scented couch, nightly embroidered with fresh flowers. With her first born nestling to her bosom— unfastening her hipband in the soft blue charms of night— she fell asleep awaiting the hour when, wrapped in clouds of love, the dreams of life would rain upon her. Yet the Prince did not come to kindle her passion's low-lit flame to seas of lambent fire, for the night of destiny had fallen, which parted him forever from independent will and common joys, to search on supermundane roads perfection in this world. Before meandering forth on moon-steeped paths, the Prince yearned to embrace both mother and child once more; albeit, afraid of awakening them, he merely threw— in the flickering light of the softly swinging lamp—a last glance of farewell and love on all his happiness. The Princess, awakening under the silvery streaks of dawn, finding herself alone with her child beneath the cover of purple and pearl, uncaressed by his delicate roaming hand, sank into a swoon. And though her soft waved limbs recovered weary life, her flower soul was dead to all its former charms. Outside the imposing castle gate, faithful Chandaka mournfully returned, leading his master's fiery steed, neighing loud. It was trapped with golden network and a saddle cloth blazened with gold and irisated with gems of every fascination, the work of the Princess. But the Prince had become a penniless and despised pilgrim, a homeless self-exile, in search for truth. [*Exit.*]

GAUTAMA [*murmurs*].   Yasodhara! —Yasodhara! He who has renounced this is no longer of earthly mould. He is past harm, even if convictions fall away and faith leave him!

[*Magic silence. The moon rises like a golden chalice from the sea of night.*]

CURTAIN

The Cave of Dawn

SCENE: *To the left, a cave, hollowed out in a steep rock. A path consisting of roughly hewn steps passes its entrance. To the right, a magnificent view on the plains, where aurora is struggling with the mist.*

THE FIVE HOLY DISCIPLES, *emaciated, with a facial resemblance to Hugo, Whitman, Tolstoi, etc., squat on deer-skins under the arch of the cave's entrance. They have a calm and self-chastised expression, as if they had written the world's history.*

SECOND DISCIPLE [*eating some herbs and sprouts*]. Here, brother.

FIRST DISCIPLE. Thanks, brother. I put a bag of fertile soil on my stomach only yesterday. It will nourish me for a while. I like to be considerate to all parts of my body and not annoy my bowels unnecessarily.

FIFTH DISCIPLE. True, my wise brother, I have not moved from this spot for three entire months.

FIRST DISCIPLE. I sometimes did not breathe for hours.

FOURTH DISCIPLE [*nods*]. What wonderful control we have over ourselves. Stupid humanity would not believe that we have touched neither man nor woman for twenty years.

FIRST DISCIPLE. And never eaten cooked food.

SECOND DISCIPLE. And waited for the rain to take a drink.

THIRD DISCIPLE. Believe me, by appropriating what we renounce, we become thus pure and strong.

FOURTH DISCIPLE. Do not let us talk so much!

FIFTH DISCIPLE. You are right, brother; let us join voices in our morning service, and then meditate on the one great word.

THE FIVE HOLY DISCIPLES [*point below and murmur, repeating each sentence three times*]. Vanity! Vanity! Vanity! Stupid, stupid humanity! We, the five only genuine holy disciples of the great Buddha, we do not believe ourselves the center of the universe. We trust nothing, like and dislike nothing, we desire nothing but to lose our individuality, to dissolve body and soul into Nirvana.

[GAUTAMA *appears, ascending the steps. Although the disciples have not seen their master for more than twenty years, they show no sign of curiosity.*]

FIRST DISCIPLE [*as* GAUTAMA *approaches*]. Bless you, who made a holy disciple out of a proud despot!

SECOND DISCIPLE. Bless you, who proved to the quondam robber chief that the life of the freest libertine on earth is nothing to that enjoyed by a holy disciple!

THIRD DISCIPLE. Bless you, who prevented a brothel-keeper from further wallowing in the mire!

FOURTH DISCIPLE. Bless you, who taught me the insufficiencies of science, the bliss of uninfluenced monology!

FIFTH DISCIPLE. Bless you, who convinced me that out and inward pain can be overcome by oblivious contemplation!

GAUTAMA. Bless you, and follow me to deny your faith!

[THE FIVE HOLY DISCIPLES *open their eyes and mouths wide.*]

GAUTAMA [*gives each a few hairs of his beard as objects of worship and smiles serenely as he proceeds on his journey*].

Follow me to deny your faith! [*He sneezes as he turns around the corner.*]

[THE FIVE HOLY DISCIPLES *toss about in hysterical despair.*]

CURTAIN

At the Boundary of Perpetual Snow

SCENE: *Moonrise o'er mountain peaks, cleaving the mist—which ghost-like floats hither and thither—in various forms and height.* GAUTAMA *is reclining on the highest pinnacle. In the distance glimmers the glacial architecture of the Himalaya.*]

GAUTAMA. Departed spirits of my faith once more, like the majestic moon, rise and move in mighty waves the ocean of my thoughts that lay at rest; not to the tempestuous fury of the past that drove resistless everything before its mighty course, and shattered human creeds like wrecks—merely a last glance of farewell at thy everlasting rise and fall, the grand monotony of life!

Oh, universe within universe, the enigma of thy existence is not cruel, not obscure to me though it has oft tormented me with sleepless agony. A repetition, nothing else: —a ceaseless play of billows of the same chaotic mass!

Just as this body's imperishable dust incessantly rebuilds the phenomena of life, reason and feeling both consist of multitudinous minute forces that, in continual transformation, attract or repulse, inflame or chill, condense or dissolve each other. These forces, wedded to the dust, roam dormant through the universe, until affinity lets them concuss to minor images of the majestic revolution: man.

All the nomadic population of water, earth and air, swarming in flocks or straying alone, even beings too small for the eye of science, all growing things, the flowers indeed,

109

nay, this solid rock, possess soul-atmospheres in inferior states. Incessant concussion during millenniums had to *in* and *e*volutionize, before the breathing of a tenuous leaf became the breath of human eloquence, before acranic two-holed bellies moved to the highest phase of individual consciousness: a mechanism even freer than the stars that can reflect upon its action and partly influence itself. The human soul with its panurgic zest and obsequious intervals of lethian rest, from where it comes, for which it pines in apathetic absentations of itself, straying through the weird capricious confusions of dreamland, or struggling in somber estuaries of insanity's sea!

By parents, manifold and cruel, the germs of our life are shed in the fields of infancy and youth; changing their substances ceaselessly, each turgescent plant, fed by all affinity can draw from chaos' surging sea, unfolds unwillingly its individual zest with soaring trunk and leafy wilderness; its fruitage falling more or less complete according to the skill, that curbs the fire fluids as they intercourse. There are souls swooning away as noonday love and glare dissolve their overheated sheath; and there are others, burning fiercely in calm intensity, until the inward fire has consumed the mortal web maintaining it.

How frail and fugitive is life! Oh, magic friend, thy vernal radiance caresses the outlines of this wasted form, still garrulous with itself as in the nights of yore, —a repetition of remembered love.

So circling time reiterates the tasks of nations and of men. Soul forces of ancestral times, currenting in unknown spheres, spinning in rhythmical curves, perchance, around some sun and influencing other conscious growths, suddenly return to human habitations to reflect the vice and glory of dead ages. Still sapient men of science ponder how reveries of sounds or color spread like pestilence through public taste.

Ye, forgemen of futurity, who will desolate your accidental sways as sages, warriors, and martyrs, how much, as I preceding captors, you'll resemble me—before whom other buddhas darken as the stars' variegation before the greenish yellow of the sun. [*Laughs softly.*] Our pabulation consisted of the same magnetic forces that command the instincts of the human herd.

Sensitive persons, —lovers of thy perlaceous pallidity, mate of my vanished dreams—in foolish weakness or emotion deep as the sundering white and dark blue sea, never overcome the loss of friendship and of love, because the soul of the departed one has left in them a part whose love lures cannot be extinguished; again, again, tenaciously they call when crushed by joyful hours or the healing antidotes of time.

As the visage of a child reflects the faces it has seen, elective pairs remaining lovers, grow alike in manner and construction as in the realm of reason and susceptibilities, for already in their first meeting, through a word or glance, a movement of the body or the soul, they shoot into each other a restless longing to complete each other in that sublime concussion which produces birth, the creative talent of the mob.

But ye, poor world-wide artists, fashioned in heaven and hell, you have absorbed too deep a share of universal heat! Its vehement radiation must repulse the multitude. Do ordinary mortals ever fathom the hungry depths of a creative soul!—perchance, in sunbeam hours of maternal sacrifice, in twilight broodings of despair, or nights of jealous rage. Life's gorges are too shallow for intensity of joy in pain; its waters, rebelling, rush to unknown limits and, inundating, rise into oblivion. I pilgered lonesome through this desert-dream, and now sit solitary on this mountain peak beyond myself.

Temple of redemption, redundant with bardic melodies

of form, the rainbow's fragrant measures, with monuments of thought, and odorous hues of sound, thy white and sacred messengers of faith, rising phoenix-like from beauty's sacred flames, sun-soaring, resuscitate with every beat of wings the inspiration of thy Artist Gods! Their deeds redeem mortality, in their time-outliving power to vibrate the imponderable into the inner world of man; and scattered love, throughout the universe transfigured, draws all affinities beneath her despot ban.

Who knows if one spark cannot call its brother from the stars with a decillion-fold rapidity of light!

Oh, thousand moments—in a high strung life—of exquisite joyful pain, can you redeem the other plight, the blank monotony over which the unconscious sheds its sere sardonic light! It is in vain, it is in vain the parasites of earth must wander forth to bane in endless discontent the inconsistencies of fate.

Even devotion, wooed by necessity and circumstance, lets her convictions glide away, time-pleasing considers them from other centers, until suddenly, in the tenebrious hour of death, doubt darts to the surface with appalling vehemence, breaking through all the stratas of persuasion and appeasement which have overgrown it, and reestablishes the old faith triumphant on waning lips.

In the final restoration, that queer riddle, which in curious trepidation all to solve solicit, old age, disease, or accident: the trinity of death loosens some threads of life's variegated web; the broken garment falls, the shivering soul dissolves, and currents of invisible sparks, forever dead, forever living, flow slumbering from sleep to sleep.

And so, what men call history, ever onward thunders: one life is launched, the other sinks, generations come and go, new nations blossom forth and rot, new worlds are born and die, new agencies of existence may originate when forces conquer consciousness without.—Come, mists, in tender wildness also wrap this solitary peak within your ghostly veils.

. . . .

. . . . It is growing cold! Yasodhara, let me fold Nirvana's mantle around your moon-lit shoulders.

[*The mists wind higher and higher, until all peaks have disappeared and the scene appears like a nebulous sea, on whose distant shore the summits of the Himalaya glow like a huge crystallized fairy castle.*]

CURTAIN

SCENE XI

Summit of the Himalaya

SCENE: [*Summit of the Himalaya. Its imposing peaks are sharply outlined against the bluish-black sky. Snow whisperings.*]

GAUTAMA [*with long, white, flowing hair and beard, in a plain white garment, enters this scene of white. It begins to snow*]. At last! At last! As far and near as human beings can approach forgetfulness on earth. . . . . Nothing . . . . sinks into Everything. . . . . Deep under me, wrapped in the misty garments of everlasting night, lies human vanity. . . . . On this altar of untrodden snow I now deny my faith, the only thing I trusted here on earth.

This mighty urn, from which the sublimest of all renunciations flows, what is it but an empty cavity through which chaos' lawless currents howl to unknown measures. Human thoughts—a hand of snow—like fragile flowers dreaming forlorn on rigid, icy heights, destined to die if they relume in other spheres. Perhaps you understand me better than I you. How can I ever know what agitations thrill through this white conglomeration at my feet! —Beyond this universe, embracing infinite eternity with every spot in space as center, may there not be beyond the outermost, beyond the innermost, somewhere, Something creating worlds without

114

the laws that men consider there. . . . .
. . . .
. . . . Come, Deodunga, tear your labyrinthian roots of fire
out from this vainglorious earth, to evanescent fragments
shattered; soar as my crystal chariot into space, with sun
and moon as fleeting steeds, with reins of stars in bridle
hand, and comets for darkness breaking whip, cleave this
paltry universe in two, revealing realms man never knew!
. . . .
[*It begins to snow more heavily.* —GAUTAMA *lies down to
sleep upon the snow.*]
. . . .
Death, gentle death, queen of beauty, benefactress of
mankind, come with thy soft, white wing and fondly fold
me in thy arms. Since my birth I often felt thy cool,
refreshing breath fanning my weary limbs, but cruel thou
always passedst by and left me to my earthly sufferings.
Now, at last I can rest at thy white breast and slumber
peacefully without hope and dreams. . . . .
. . . .
This is the end; the momentary trance will cease; the
dream of soul inflations from god's bourn has past. . . . I
may awake to something else which I have never left as I
was never here. It was a play, ridiculous and sad, enacted in
my whimful self. . . . . . All is non existent.
[*Snowstorm.*]
. . . . Body and soul, farewell for ever! If you can,
impregnate other unconscious melodies with boundless
bliss. . . . .
. . . .
[*Gusts of snowflakes move to and fro, weaving a winding sheet
for* BUDDHA, *under which he disappears from the eyes of
humanity, like all of us, one after the other, as if we had never
existed.*]

CURTAIN

Darkness in Space

TO STUDENTS OF COLOR PSYCHOLOGY: *Poetical license imagines that, at* BUDDHA'S *entering Nirvana, a color revery takes place in the universe. This scene, a concert of self-radiant colors, is to be represented by pyrotechny, brought by chemistry, electricity and future light-producing sciences to such perfection and beauty that it becomes the new Optic Art, in which Color will rival Sound as a vehicle of pure emotion.*

SCENE: *Bluish-black darkness in space: a minute section of the universe, represented by a stage of at least 800 yards length and 500 yards height and depth.*

I. Out of darkness the earth, in the ban of the sun and followed by her pallid paramour the moon, ever revolving rolls majestically forward, displaying the phenomena of a lunar and solar eclipse, and growing larger and larger until she has become so large that one can discern: the ultramarine of the oceans, the glaucous of the steppes, the pallid gold of the deserts, the crystal fretwork of the poles and glaciers, and here and there the dark flyspecks of the largest cities, which become scintillant as the other colors fade in earthly night. It impresses the beholder like the colossal ideal of human vanity and then rolls backwards into darkness.

II. Confused tumbling of meteors through space—a symbol of man's life, propelled from some unknown bourn and rushing to some unknown goal, proving its momentary existence merely by a luminous line, lit and extinguished without change of course. The meteors, varying continually in the rhythm of entrance and exit, mobility, richness and intensity of fire, shoot forth in every direction, also in every possible angle, towards the audience.

III. Incessant rain of luminous stellar dust, in the midst of which a battle of stars, comets, planets with rings and satellites, takes place. They rush towards each other, and recede, encircle each other and create endless variations of figures. Now and then stars crush into each other with a great explosion of fire, unite into larger stars and, continuing their course, emit a light produced by a combination of their colors when separate. Suddenly the stars grow larger and larger, the smaller ones disappearing behind the larger, until a few dozens have reached the diameter of 50 yards, who in turn repeat a crescendo of concussions. An orange and a blue star collide and form a still larger one radiating a greenish light of painful hope. A roseate and blue star also collide to a violet glow of melancholy bliss. Thereupon these two collide, and before they grow into one, all the other stars crush into them, causing an incandescent firebrand that radiates the entire space with its irisating light. This fire wall is suddenly cleft in two, and in innumerable hues and palpitations melts away in "diminuendo."

IV. The lower (1/4) part of the stage represents the sea of chaos over which by some caprice the light effects of an earthly day, from a bloodred dawn to a moonlit night, are performed in color gradations of subtlest purity, accompanied by descriptive music.

Intermezzo, entitled "Alhambra Arabesques." In succession the famous patterns in luminous gold, blue and faded red, interlace, overlap, and link each other before the eyes of the audience, and finally change into an improvisation of new designs of the same character. (For other intermezzos the author suggests "The Shattered Jewel Casket," "Flowers growing in Cloudland," etc.)

117

V. A kaleidoscopical symphony of color effects continu-ally changing in elation and depression, velocity, intensity, variety and sentiment, continually developing and compos-ing new forms and designs, not merely of mathematical symmetry, but also as suggested from the endless construc-tions, textures, phenomena revealed in astronomy, micros-copy, mineralogy, geology, paleontology, etc., beginning with a *Lhargetto* in light bluish-grey, muddy yellowish-green, greenish-blue and dark greyish-blue; followed by an *Andante* in color containing blue from green to purple; by an *Allegretto* ofcomplimentary colors with a tendency towards yellow and red; and by a *Finale vivace* in all colors, ending at last with a flower star, emitting rocket like fire lines, trills, radiations of various propelling power, at first paraphrasing in the colors of the solar spectrum, and at last improvising an outburst of new colors, like ultra red and violet, for which optical instruments have first to be invented before the human eye can perceive and enjoy them.

Christ

A Dramatic Poem in Three Acts

(Written 1889-1891)

Persons Represented

JESHUA
MOTHER MARIA, *his mother*
MAGDALEN, *his sister*
    Brothers and sisters to Jeshua
AN OLD HERMIT
TUBAL CAIN, *a money-dealer*
HANNAH, *a pilgrimess*
EVA, *a young widow*
AHOLIBAH ⎫
TABEA   ⎬   *young girls of the village*
HAGAR   ⎭
ELLOSAR, *a poet*
OTHNIEL ⎫
REUBEN ⎬   *young men of the village*
SEMAJA   ⎭
    Men, women, children, temple-guard, etc.
CARUS MAXIMUS, *a Roman centurion*
    Roman soldiers
ZENOBIA, *a foreign queen*
PRINCE PARSONDES
CAMILLUS, *a Greek, her steward*
ATMA, *a dancing-woman*
    *Cortege of Zenobia and Parsondes, stewards, male and
        female attendants, body-guard, amazons, musicians,
        palanquin-bearers, etc.*

121

Synopsis

ACT I

SCENE: *To the left* MOTHER MARIA'S *cottage. A road leads across the stage. In the background a well. View on the sandhills.*

TUBAL CAIN [*enters with* MOTHER MARIA]. Nobody is impatient with his creditors, Mother Maria. As I have said before, my demands you must meet. Old Tubal Cain may be pot-bellied and bandy-legged, but he is not such a fool as to wait until the next festive year, he, he!

MOTHER MARIA [*leaning on a staff*]. You only open your mouth to speak evil.

TUBAL CAIN. The poor can easily be generous. The rich have to be brutal now and then. Yet we two will remain friends, won't we, Mother Maria?

MOTHER MARIA. The desire of gain has no true friends.

TUBAL CAIN. Yet its power is omnipotent —How is Jeshua? It seems to me that he brings nothing but bitterness upon her who bore him.

MOTHER MARIA. True, he never lends a helping hand in all our distress, and yet he is my favorite son. Sorrow is often the comfort of old age.

TUBAL CAIN. He does not labor, aye? Labor warms the body; he who does not work deserves his poverty.

MOTHER MARIA. He was born for something better. I, his own mother, have never understood the motive of his life. He is different to other human beings.

TUBAL CAIN. No matter whether a goat be white or black, it should give the same amount of milk. That is an old saying. Things learnt in childhood are not forgotten.

MOTHER MARIA. Then remember your mother; she never spoke an unkind word to anyone.

TUBAL CAIN. I remember my mother well, he, he. When a child, I laughingly grasped with my little fingers for the glittering coins, which she was clinking in her hand to please me. Gold rules this world. An ass who denies it.

MOTHER MARIA. Cursed be the man who first brought gold among his fellow men. It dries up every source of kindness and affection.

TUBAL CAIN. Mammon is a lust of possession, and so is love. Like all human efforts it contains as much good as evil. Without these gerahs we would have no temple in Jerusalem, no caravans bringing to us the luxuries of the East and West—no progress could take place. And those who willingly denounce wealth in words would be the very ones to misuse it, if they could, he, he.

MOTHER MARIA. But to what purpose do you toil and struggle? Your gold creates no beneficial influence. Avarice is no enjoyment.

TUBAL CAIN. If you would but consent to make my dwelling yours, you would value my frugality.

MOTHER MARIA. Be silent—not another word!

TUBAL CAIN. I or another man, what is the difference as long as one is wholesome?

MOTHER MARIA. To insult a woman is an easy task, Tubal Cain.

TUBAL CAIN. Gossip says so, not I. I like you; that's all. I like stout women. Yes, I do, he, he.

MOTHER MARIA. I have loved but once.

TUBAL CAIN. But he was not your husband?

MOTHER MARIA. To the carpenter I was married against my will. It was adultery. I have loved but once. The sun shone hot upon me, but the golden light did not linger upon my head. Like a day of pleasure, it quickly passed.

[*As to herself.*] One evening, standing out there in the desert, I mourned and longed for him who had left me for a hermit's life. I felt as if I were alone—alone in this wide, barren world. All springs of nature were at rest; neither bird nor insect seemed to live. All bright colors were lost in the darkness pervading the silent, desolate plain. Time itself stood still, as if hesitating to lift the veil from the immensity of that lonely, immeasurable stretch of sand, where hitherto, only the spirits of perished nations swayed in deep lament. It was a silence which my presence seemed to desecrate. An inexpressible fear came over me—a dream of heavenly love stormed o'er my trembling frame. I saw my lover's pale, wan face in clouds of raining light, and my maternal fruitfulness embraced the seed of Jeshua. [*She stands at the garden gate, in Titanic gloom after her short summer life, like the personification of the Jewish race—a picture, stern and sombre, like the Arabian desert.*]

TUBAL CAIN.   Nature cannot be overcome. We all admire purity. It is our body that causes disturbances. We all err through our temperament. Yes, yes, Mother Maria, love is a burden.

MOTHER MARIA.   It is a cruelty to women wherever unlawful maternity is proclaimed a crime. As long as a woman's body glows with the warmth of youth, men will be desirous to test her amativeness. To him it becomes the memory of a radiant hour of joy; while the woman is obliged to suckle a being of whom she owns nothing but the burden and the shame.

TUBAL CAIN.   You speak of free copulation, I of marriage.

MOTHER MARIA.   Wedlock is but free copulation sanctioned by the law, nothing more. Leave me for tonight, good Tubal Cain. [*Turns to exit.*]

TUBAL CAIN [*shrugs his shoulders; aside*].   How I would like to pet her haunches! [*Exits slowly.*]

125

JESHUA [*enters, robed in dull red*].   Mother, what are your
dealings with this man?

MOTHER MARIA.   Those which necessity demand. [*Looks
at Jeshua with a yearning expression.*]

JESHUA.   Mother?

MOTHER MARIA.   My son, why do you act so strangely?
People speak of you in a slandering way. They say that you
intend renouncing the Mosaic laws. Remember, you are a
Jew, even if your father was a stranger to this land. Do not
take vengeance upon me and my great sin by casting aside
the religion of my forefathers.

JESHUA.   Mother, have I ever said a word of reproach to
you?

MOTHER MARIA.   No, Jeshua.

JESHUA.   Why then, Mother, must our roads always cross
each other?

MOTHER MARIA.   I would do anything, my son, to please
you. [*Aside.*] Can I do nothing to draw him to me? [*Exits.*]

JESHUA.   Shall I ever be understood? The world is so
wide, and I am alone! The world is so wide!—oh, years
without fulfillment! how I suffer, wasting my energies of
youth! In hours of adversity I also grow faithless like the
rest.

[*Occupies himself in the garden.*]

ELLOSAR [*enters in conversation with* OTHNIEL, REUBEN,
and SEMAJA].   Day for day, my whole being concentrates
itself in a long, lascivious, lambent breath of longing! How
can these amorous sighs be satisfied? Youth is troublesome
enough without sterility.

OTHNIEL.   Virgins, for various reasons, are as inconvenient as lewds. Childless widows and cunning jades seem
most commendable.

REUBEN.   The guide through all sexual temptations
should be health, and health alone.

SEMAJA.   Oh, let nature have its way; we can in nowise

126

improve upon it. [*Points to* EVA.] A wind-stirred garment reveals to men all there is and can ever be.

ELLOSAR. True enough. I feel as if dewdrops should impearl her lanuginous chalice of hope. Oh, garden of defloration, what loveless denudations have swept through thy mystic realms!

JESHUA. Innocence in manly strength should consecrate each sexual kiss with salutary gentleness.

OTHNIEL [*to* SEMAJA]. In such company, it were best to be a hermaphrodite.

ELLOSAR. Virtue can only be based on knowledge and conviction. The innocent and ignorant can neither be chaste nor sensual.

JESHUA. Self-denial in love's desire, however fierce or faint it may be!

ELLOSAR. Dear friend, you speak of self-denial and know not what it is. The pregnant lines in which a woman is created would also weave a magic web around your soul while resting in a virgin's arm.

[JESHUA *smiles.*]

OTHNIEL. Oh, abstinent Essenian! For you must know that Jeshua is more modest than a sister of Ammon behind her curtain.

ELLOSAR. And you, wanton Saducee, cannot let a woman pass without insulting and undressing her in your imagination.

OTHNIEL. Can you?

REUBEN [*musingly*]. Jeshua and Othniel are two entirely different representatives of life, and yet alike. Neither will fathom fatherhood.

SEMAJA [*to* JESHUA]. And do you never feel as if you should purify yourself in the ardent glow of a deep delight?

[JESHUA *remains silent.*]

REUBEN. You see how natures differ. Othniel, you never knew restraint without dictation. Look at the Arabs, how they breed their horses. They do not allow the stallion to touch the mare after conception, while husbands molest their wives a few hours before delivery.

OTHNIEL. Should they mount their neighbor's mare, perhaps?

ELLOSAR. If men and women would practice purity in married life, what a glorious religion would rise from the present chaos! Science and philosophy, music and poetry, all arts, all noble, unselfish actions would be the children of one mother: Health.

OTHNIEL. When will that be?

ELLOSAR. The future will proudly assert that the seminal fluid of a perfect father is the very essence of life, and that upon the wombs of perfect mothers the happiness of the world depends. Sexual intercourse could be a religion! The wife, trembling with the hopes of maternity, embraces with all her trust and feminine grandeur her husband, who presses all his strength, his manliness, and ideal thought into her sacred body. Such a connection between body and body, soul and soul, is worthy of god—the creation of life, the eternity of nature, divinity itself!

OTHNIEL. If you were god, how different the world would be. [*Murmurs.*] For my part, Aholibah suits my loins well enough.

SEMAJA. Such idle imaginings remain a blank to me.

REUBEN. It is a pastime. But who comes there?

SEMAJA. The old centurion, who has half persuaded me to join the Roman army.

CARUS MAXIMUS [*enters with soldiers and a crowd of villagers*]. Flock around the Roman eagle, boys! Show courage! Take the chance I offer you. Ovations and trophies shall be yours. Do not hesitate; enter a life of liberty! Nothing more glorious than a life of war!

JESHUA. Will mankind never lead a peaceful life?

CARUS MAXIMUS. Never, youth. War is a necessity;

peace unnatural. What would become of man if he could not endure the sight of blood and death? What would become of valor, vigor, vassalage? They soon would have to sound retreat, and power would fall to the vafrous. I spent many years at Augustus' imperial court, unrolled many a parchment scroll, witnessed the devotions of many creeds, gazed at the triumphs of beauty in Rome and in foreign lands, but nothing met my eye that could rival this keen-edged sword. Rather a scabrous gladiator than a decrepit sage! To me, he is a god who knows no fear! Who will enlist?

SEMAJA. Put down my name! I have nothing to lose and much to gain.

YOUNG MEN. Also mine! —And mine! —Would I had no filial piety to perform! —Alas, that I am still so young!

CARUS MAXIMUS. Brave, my boys! You will never repent it. Blow the bugle! strike the drum! We march tomorrow. Now go, and enjoy the last evening at home; and let sweethearts and sisters decorate my future heroes with garlands of flowers. [*Exits with soldiers and young men, who shout and embrace each other.*]

[*Young girls and women come with jars and vessels to the well,* TABEA *and* HAGAR *among them.*]

HERMIT [*crosses the stage*]. I once dreamed like you, my boys. I also loved the burning sun; now, I prefer a clear and mellow evening. The feeling of approaching darkness and melancholy solitude of night, puts my mind at rest. All your strength, imagination, ardent zeal of youth, will arrive at the same goal. And as annihilation knows of no restraint, the nations which you conquer, as well as the Roman empire which you serve, will perish. At last all humanity will decay. Sun and stars will extinguish; like this day, the earth will sink into oblivion.

TABEA. She will soon be here. I long to see her.

AHOLIBAH [*enters with* EVA; *a mysterious, sensual smile plays continually about* AHOLIBAH'S *lips, she is dressed in green*

129

and black]. Are you speaking of the foreign queen? I am craving to know, how many of her suitors the enchantress has killed.

TABEA. Her camp equipments passed by this morning. At least thirty camels, accompanied by hundreds of slaves.

HAGAR. Why are some people so poor and others so rich?

AHOLIBAH. There is no greater harlot living; they say, she changes her lovers as we change our robes.

TABEA. That takes away all my pleasure of seeing her.

AHOLIBAH. You need not stay. The loom and spindle are waiting for you at home. [*Aside.*] Oh, if I could but lead her wild, unrestrained life! Oh, that there are thousands of men longing for us, and that we dare not satisfy them and ourselves. The thought drives me mad. Why is this forbidden and that not allowed? If it is wrong, why am I so created that at certain moments I feel like throwing myself into the arms of the lowest man?

EVA. Hush!

MOTHER MARIA [*sings inside the cottage*]. Unhappy children, having lost a parent still mother-naked, children growing up in ignorance and want, children bred without a kind word or kiss.

Toil along, toil along!

Unhappy lovers, young widows and widowers, parents sitting at the empty cradle, beggars, all diseased and deformed beings, poets and artists without success,

Toil along, toil along!

Unhappy mortals, struggling with poverty, sickness and sorrow, repentant sinners, all human beings who have a crime on their conscience,

Toil along, toil along, oh, toil along!

ELLOSAR. Look at the last greeting of the setting sun! What color-dreams weave over the distant hills! The evening star steals softly into the trembling air. [*The temple-guard is heard singing.*] Heaven on earth! That my art could

130

hold this picture for eternity! But before we have comprehended it, it fades in its magic flight.

OTHNIEL. Ellosar, write a song on these colors, so hot and so wild!

REUBEN. The golden dust can be seen, but not grasped.

ELLOSAR. Always denying?

REUBEN. Always searching for truth.

ELLOSAR. And never admiring when it reveals itself.

TABEA. How wide the meshes of the spider's web are. A sure sign of bad weather.

AHOLIBAH. I dissolve in pain. [*The languid voluptuousness of Southern climes takes possession of her body.*]

[EVA *in profound silence watches the sunset. Jeshua comes into the garden and saws wood.*]

TABEA. Look at Jeshua.

AHOLIBAH. He pretends to be above curiosity.

EVA. Jeshua always acts as he feels.

OTHNIEL [*to* AHOLIBAH]. You spoke quite differently about him last summer, if I do not err?

AHOLIBAH. We sometimes change and know not why.

HAGAR. In my life, nothing changes. One day is like the other, full of pain.

[HANNAH *enters barefooted; she perceives* JESHUA, *and stands as if in a dream; the languid voluptuousness of Southern climes takes for a moment possession of her soul.*]

TABEA. Queer I could never understand Jeshua.

OTHER GIRLS. Nor I! —Nor I!

AHOLIBAH. What is there strange about it? Is he not the son of Mother Maria? Sons take after their mother. [*Aside.*] God forgive me for saying this. How I have loved that man! Milk exuded from my nipples from very joy, when I thought of him. And he rejected me!

EVA. Jeshua deserves everyone's love.

TABEA. There they come! [*Music is heard, slaves appear waving perfumed kerchiefs and strewing flowers, carmine, and*

131

gold dust on the road. Coins are thrown among the crowd, who shout Hosanna!]

JESHUA. So everybody is saluted, whether friend or foe, as long as curiosity is satisfied. [*Enter* CAMILLUS *and attendants, some on horse back.* ZENOBIA, *dressed in striped black and golden yellow, is borne on a palanquin.* PRINCE PARSONDES *rides in a chariot. The village girls hail them with palm leaves.*]

PARSONDES. What a vile place!

ZENOBIA. We shall linger here over night.

PARSONDES. In your embrace the humblest spot on earth converts into a place of bliss.

MURMURING OF THE CROWD. Isn't she just splendid! —She looks like the queen of abomination!—What sumptuous, saturated brilliancy! —What merciless glare and glitter!—Not half as dazzling as I thought! —Observe the luring glances of her emerald eye! —I wonder if the vermilion of her lips is real! —How grey those many-colored tunics look! —Will I be able to hallow her after-image by my art?

ZENOBIA. How they stare at me! I am used to the shouting of multitudes. Soulless creatures, insipid fools, they envy me, and do not know that I am the unhappiest creature of them all. In my mighty passion I absorb all other ones. I stand smiling in the arena of the world, and shed my heart-blood unseen, in the carmine and gold dust of my poetry. [*Suddenly perceives* JESHUA, *and stares at him.* HANNAH *anxiously watches the queen.*]

CAMILLUS. What ails you, my queen?

ZENOBIA. Find out the name of yonder swain.

CAMILLUS [*aside*]. May the gods of your forefathers preserve you from her luring smiles, young Jew.

ZENOBIA. I have never met the man of whom I desired children until now. Embracing him I could fall into eternal slumber. And mine he will be. An ocean of light surrounds

132

me. Oh, could I but throw myself into its clear and steady flames, that it might purify and burn up all that is foul within me!

AHOLIBAH. She has cast an eye upon the coyish dreamer. Ha! wait now and see, if he can resist that virulent demon of passion.

HANNAH. I knew it, I knew it! [ZENOBIA *and procession exit; the crowd follows them. A few remain, speaking about the event, then slowly disperse in different directions. Only* HAN- NAH *and* JESHUA *remain on the stage. It grows dark during the following scene.*]

HANNAH [*slowly approaches* JESHUA, *and whispers with sisterly affection*]. Beware! Beware!

[*Long pause.*]

JESHUA. Who are you?

HANNAH. A part of you. All else I love in you. Take what I am, it is yours!

JESHUA. Who are you?

HANNAH. I know no more, I simply feel that I belong to you, and to nobody else on earth.

[*They gaze at each other for a long while, then embrace.*]

JESHUA. The first long, slumbering kiss confirms all that god and the heavens decreed.

HANNAH [*quivering with bliss*]. Hold me fast!

[*Pause.*]

JESHUA. Also upon us lingers the silent sadness known to all who listen to the woeful song of life and death. We soar above the dust and bitterness of human cares. When our lips meet, they touch—

HANNAH. Infinitude.

JESHUA. Infinitude. Our Love is as healthy and strong as the noon of summer days. Ages may sink into the past, yet our friendship would not change, not even with death, for we would continue—

HANNAH. Beyond.

JESHUA. Beyond. The waves of our mind meet on the vibrating ocean of air, and wandering to and fro, from soul to soul, call forth responsive thoughts.

BOTH [*as in a trance, hardly audible,* HANNAH *speaking more softly than* JESHUA, *like music accompanying a song.*]. Our Love fills the world with the thunder of unearthly joy! We penetrate into all the kindred parts of the universe. Like eagles, we cleave the ambient realms of dark and darker blue, and break the dreariness of Northern darkness as inconstant lights. We sweep over vast, variegated plains, and sink with the roaring waters into the depth of the wild, unresting sea!

How glorious is our Love! We float with the jubilating songs of nightingales on the silver beams of night. We rest on the lips of lovers; we bloom with the flowers that fade unseen, and smile through the mist of tears at morn. We rest on Nature's bosom, and dream her naked dream of grace; we feel the burning passion of all mankind, and the body becomes as sacred as the soul!

How old and new is our Love! We are buried by hurricanes that crush the homes of peaceful men; we drown in seas of blood shed for a future state of joy. And, with enthusiasm's blazing flames our Love soars to the suns of heaven, and falls into the sunless gulfs of hell. We leap into the boundlessness of space, and taste, in the rapture of one moment, the eternity of time!

We laugh at the violence of fate; we laugh at wealth, wisdom, beauty, power. We sink into each other's arms. Dark immensity of night surround us! We are in Love! [*In their kisses, body and soul are trembling in a rapturous embrace.*]

The heavens open! The widening infinite! Spirits of heaven and hell, they cast their sickles upon earth, and stars are falling from the clouds, and earthquakes split the realms, and still we cry for Love, more Love!

And from the unfathomed depth of this restless world

rise thousands of gigantic visions. We tremble in the laments of life; we feel the holy agony, the godlike sufferings of the past; and our bodies crumble into dust, while our souls mount to those wonderful, brooding stars, which flame through the sky in endless variation.

[*An old* HERMIT *enters.*]

Oh, everchanging orbs of God, you are the symbol of Love! Myriads of falling stars, that whirl around each other, you are like the maddening yearning of humanity itself; the nameless longing of life and Love to throw itself into another life and Love, until you dash together in the fury of a glorious, overwhelming light! [*Meteors shoot across heaven.*]

HERMIT. Oh, world of fire-balls, destined to be embodied in one star, in you mankind can read, night for night, the secret of the universe, how glowing suns transform into cold and glittering stars of ice, till they collide to become once more the ardent suns of time and space. And like creation's cycling course the stars form circles, rolling forth in endless chains to nothingness. The fires of the universe prophecy their destiny in your immortal Love, [*Extends his arms to* HANNAH *and* JESHUA.] when at last, in the far-distant future, all the ambitious suns of heaven tumble into one mighty, burning giant star, who will shed a light of redemption over the final union of hostile elements, sleeping mysteriously and motionless in the dark immensity of time. Then Love, the one colossal soul of the departed worlds, will dreamingly begin a new existence for decillions of ages to come. [*The old* HERMIT *exits, the lovers remain as petrified, in an embrace expressing the triumph of purity in Love. The stars are sparkling like diamonds on the turquoise vault. After a long pause, the curtain drops.*]

ACT II

Scene I

SCENE: *An interior of* MOTHER MARIA'S *cottage. The deep violet light of dawn streams through the windows.* JESHUA'S *brothers and sisters sleep picturesquely grouped on mats, divans, and cushions, around a hearth of clay.*

JESHUA [*dreaming a morning dream*].   Oh, Hannah, star of my life, you shall not go! Can it be true that even you will fade from the heaven of my hopes? Your lips are twitching with secret wishes, yet your eyes are staring in bitter hate. Let us then part! No love proves true within these whirling spheres. Farewell, grey walls of my mother's home! Farewell to the sandhills and vineyards where I have roamed in hours of careless innocence! Farewell to all the interests of youth! Farewell, beloved one; farewell to all the sacred hours, the hopeful dreams of our love!

And hail to thee, thou dismal land, where the restive joys of our past will grow to unknown fates! —It is so dark around me now. No love proves true within these whirling spheres. Yet you I must remember in all eternity.

Day and night, roll on, roll on, and sweep away my paradise of dreams! All better thoughts flee from my memory! Swift-gliding years in restless works are all that I behold.

Oh, nature, fill me with the violent energy of life! I wish to conquer and command. Now see me kneeling at the feet of those who wear the diadems of fame. I flatter them. I rise, and all their sins I own. Swift-gliding years in restless

136

works are all that I behold, and thus all former virtues turn but fugitive lights in the haunting shadows of my self. Now I am king! Woe to you all! Like sultry winds, the breath of death lolls on the plain.

Humanity make no demands on me! You speak of innocence, how it suffers in this fleeting dream; but what is that to me? Let them perish in this world of moan. Begone, with words you cannot threaten me! Away, detested race, I hate you. Do not curse me; accurse yourselves, for you have petrified my soul.

Oh, that I knew a being on whose breast I could forget that immortality is the fate of every living object on the earth! Oh, that I knew a place where I could rest when, in dark and dreary hours, the horror of loneliness steals on my weary heart! Yet all my life is vain. My soul knows love no more, and all my sufferings are eternal, creep into the infinite.

Oh, nature, you majestic queen of all, come with your storms, and let them desolate the lands! Open your deepest depth of hell, my mother earth, and take me back into thy burning lap! Fall upon me, ye proud and dazzling walls of heaven; bury the remnants of my life; oh, still under the ruins my reeling brain would feel the tortures of that thought from which is no escape!

Prophet star, thy light is fading in the purple rain of sin. Hope is dying, hope is dying, loud and louder grows the din. Blood, blood, blood through all the ages, from beginning to the end! Blood, blood, blood in every dwelling—glint of steel in clinching hand! Tears, tears, tears in every valley where the seeds of life are sown. Tears, tears, tears on every summit where a fruitful tree has grown!

Enough laments, enough of woe! Here I lie prostrate and forlorn before thy mighty throne, god of my better days; dead while living, waiting for a deathless death I pray! Hark! Hear I right? A voice is calling. "Human sins will be forgiven through your faith in Hannah's faith."

137

Oh, dreams of my youth, you golden memories of the past, help me to find my soul again! Oh, love, let sound thy melodies! Oh, morning sun of love, of first and only love, shine into my aching soul, that it may learn to hope again!

Dawn, aurora, a new life! The infinite sufferings of years are melting into tears of joy. Leave me, black night! Dark shadows, fly! Oh, slumbering world, awake! I pray to the star of immortality—to pure, unselfish love.

CURTAIN

ACT II

Scene II

SCENE: *Among the sandhills. A road leads across the stage. At the right, a view on the sublime solitude of the desert.*

HERMIT. Oh, sunshine, sunshine, how you dazzle, and spread your light upon the vast and silent plain. Here is rest from the turmoil of the world. Everywhere silence: deep, sad silence; nothing torments me; it is as if I knew everything, and was set free from all earthly bonds. And yet as I feel at my heart, and listen to its peaceful hymns, pictures of the past are rising. Once more I stand in the golden light of youth. I longingly open my arms, as I was wont to do in the days when I was young, and I clasp the empty air. The desert lies before me. The hoped for happiness was but a dream of youth. Self-improvement has taught me to accept success and failure as they come. Hope is justified through nothing on this earth, for existence is illusion, and human efforts but a grand mistake. Even the greatest success is a failure. The sage alone never fails, because he never attempts to act. So I patiently wait, until I go to those regions, where neither weal nor woe can influence us, where ideas melt into the oblivion of Nirvana: a realm of perfect peace, without even a suggestion of the absence of ideas.

JESHUA [*enters in deep meditation*]. Will I succeed?

HERMIT. My son!

JESHUA. Will I teach mankind to lead a happier life than they do now?

HERMIT. How can sorrow be extinguished by a mortal?

JESHUA. By hope in all adversity.

HERMIT. Will it give them hours of absolute serenity, undarkened by the gloom of care?

JESHUA. Yes, if all human beings considered themselves the members of one family; if we assisted each other to overcome every evil that befalls us.

HERMIT. You speak of something, that can never be ours in all lights and shades of eternity.

JESHUA. Some glorious inspiration may form mysterious clouds around me—the shadows of the greatest light.

HERMIT. Vain endeavors! The eternal light may shine, but the darkness will not comprehend it. Tell them to live without demands, and happiness will be theirs unawares. If we abandon appetites and restrain our passions, we escape all troubles and anxiety. We bring joy and pain upon ourselves. The highest phase of life is to be self-contained, immutable.

JESHUA. Who but a sage can do it? Inferiors cannot depend upon their strength alone. The reward of virtue by a higher power will give them self-enjoyment, rectitude, and peace.

HERMIT. Nature alone could do it. No promise can be more exalted than the voice which speaks in wind and water. Let nature sound its echoes in the human soul, and it will rise above nations, lands, and seas; above the world, above the stars, to search in the vast wastes of ether for its original home.

JESHUA. You are like the lily on the placid waters, sublime in mystery. Wait for the day of revelation.

HERMIT. The unknown will never be known, the unconscious will never be conscious.

JESHUA. You cannot rob me of my faith. If men and women had *no secrets* from each other, and felt that the intention is as good or bad as the deed itself, they would not hesitate to pity and pardon, to trust and assist each other.

Then love would find its final utterance in all embracing sympathy. The rest I leave to the wisdom of my people.

HERMIT. On whose help do you depend in this gigantic task?

JESHUA. I trust in myself alone.

HERMIT. A man who trusts in himself is isolated.

JESHUA. A man with new and bold ideas expects no help from others.

HERMIT. Bold youth, what is your will against that power that formed substance, life, and space from the chaos of time?

JESHUA. I know one man is nothing, fate everything, but some men become their own fate.

HERMIT. Kingdoms have fallen to ruins, the gods of old stand lonesome at their shrines, whole civilizations have been swept away in the furious run of time, the sand of the desert may swallow up all Palestine—the loving arms that embraced me in childhood have withered long ago. Why should the laws of your new faith prove irresistible? Human life is a continual up-and-down, never ending, never-changing, until everything has passed away.

JESHUA. If everything is transitory, if nothing can resist the gnawing tooth of time, if everything that our eyes behold must gradually decay, let us at least wander towards the future, hand in hand, like lovers, like brothers and sisters, like the children of one god!

HERMIT. Progress will welcome every gleam and glimmer of true light. [*Bugles sound; both listen. The Roman soldiers pass by with* SEMAJA *and other* YOUNG MEN *of the village in their ranks.*]

SEMAJA. Farewell, Jeshua! Manhood is made to wander, and so am I. God alone knows whither. My love to Recha, and a farewell to all!

[YOUNG MEN *exit, shouting and singing.*]

JESHUA [*standing on a rock. Now and then the bugles sound,*

141

gradually dying away]. God be with you! May everyone
reach satisfaction at the end. I do not envy you. True, it is
great, banner in hand, to lead an army of strong, armed
warriors to victory. To march, crowned with the laurel
wreath of fame, under triumphal arches to the Capitol! To
sit on golden thrones, and have proud foreign queens kneel
at one's feet. Alas! my road will also lead over battle fields,
with mangled, festering corpses, pass through odious seas of
stenchening blood; but it will lead to truth.

HERMIT.   And what is truth?

[JESHUA *crosses his arms on his breast, and looks up to
heaven.* HERMIT *softly shakes his head, and exits. Pause.*]

JESHUA [*prays*].   Oh, god of truth, I have listened so
often to the captious and minatious words of my brethren;
for years I have meditated if thou art truly existent, and
always with the same result—reason denies thee, feeling
affirms thee still. Oh, god of truth, thou art inexplicable!
Who dares to manifest thee? Thou art to men and women
what they should be to themselves. And yet the highest
thought to which my urgent, auguring mind can rise, art
thou: my property, nobody else's. Faith in thee is only in its
totality alike, giving to every creature a different ideal of
thy existence. —I am no Jew. —I belong to no creed. —I
belong to every one. —I endeavor to be god man. —Better
voice within myself, thou art my god! Brethren, my god is
within me. I am myself my god! [*Falling asleep, he murmurs.*]   Dark spots and sparks of fire—streaks of red—a
deluge of unknown colors—a luminous orb is drowning
fast—familiar scenes rise reddish-brown—an unseen smile
is floating by; the sin of love in a serpent eye.

[*Desert weaving.*]

ZENOBIA [*enters, dressed like the Assyrian Istar, with bow
and quiver slung over her shoulder. She makes a sign to her
female attendants to depart, then looks at* JESHUA *for a long
while before she speaks*].   Why do my knees tremble as I

loosen my girdle? Zenobia's pride has humbled the most audacious self-esteem, and shall not fail this time!

JESHUA [*raves in his dream*]. On sunny shades—creation's music—refluent waves of after-bliss—a cross is rising within the white and bluish mist—black, gigantic; it fills the universe—save one red flower climbing up the shaft, all else grows dark—and dead—also the flower breaks, and— [*Zenobia kisses* JESHUA's *mouth.*] falls upon my mouth like soft, human lips. [*He awakes.*] What fragrant dream of beauty blurs my sight? Ha! whom do I behold?

ZENOBIA. Zenobia, queen of the East! Cling to me, and leave on my lips the voluptuous breath of life, a deluge of fire, boundless desires for never-ending bliss. The yearning for an ideal existence as a curse on our head, and the wonderful flower of passion in the suffocating heat of our hearts, we wander lonesome on the shore of cold reality, extending our arms towards a home of joy, which will never be ours.

JESHUA. We two have nothing in common.

ZENOBIA. Nothing but ambition. Are not our kisses like lamentations from the depths of the earth? Are not our sighs like the hungry cry of two majestic beasts of prey, searching for glowing flesh and blood in the desert of sensation?

JESHUA. Woman, I do not understand your passion nor your sadness, for sad you are. I long for deep affection which is lasting, like the love of a mother to her child; the love of twin brothers and sisters; of the artist for his art, destined by higher decrees to mingle and be one.

ZENOBIA. Oh, listen to the flow of my tears, over the nothingness of life, in the elegies of those nights when my body can find no rest in the limitation of its sphere; when my better self is praying for an eternal sleep, in the arms of deathless joy. Then there is within me a chaos in which good and evil spirits crowd together in indescribable confusion. My body, as if possessed by madness, devoured by passions gloomy and imperishable, is in a desperate war with my better self, which strives for the serene perfection of a god.

JESHUA.   If nothing can satisfy you, what do you want of me?

ZENOBIA.   Give me peace in pleasure, and the riches of Judea shall be yours! I will make you the ruler of vast domains; nations shall kneel at your feet, and hail you king! Your name shall be carried over land and sea; it shall even reach distant Lundinium. The kings of all the world shall pay homage to you!

JESHUA.   Worldly enjoyments are valueless to me.

ZENOBIA.   Then I renounce them. [*Scatters gold.*] I tear the jewels from my limbs! [*Throws off her jewels.*] Take me as I am, I am yours!

JESHUA.   Woman, what is your aim in this? If you think of tempting me, your efforts shall prove vain.

ZENOBIA.   Oh, come to the festivals of my native land; to flower beds in enchanted groves, near shimmering lakes! There, before the sacred shrines of our shadowy gods, wrapt in clouds of incense, men and women dance to the tinkling of cymbals and the wailing of flutes. Bare shoulders and naked breasts glow in the tepid atmosphere, flowing garments are floating in an ocean of light, and myrrh and orange blossoms sink fading to the ground. How the torchlight dwells upon the half-veiled limbs! Louder and louder the music sounds, swifter and swifter the footsteps glide over the glittering sand! Look at those bacchantes! Their dark eyes—what wild desires they express—their trembling nostrils and moist, quivering lips! In emulous ardor every movement tempts with boundless bliss! Thought and feeling are forgotten, only the body lives!

JESHUA.   Cease to speak! I will listen no further.

ZENOBIA.   Oh, for the days of soft rubescence, ere my

free, fresh inflorescence was unmarred by violation's glow! The nightingales sang softly on sycamore and cypress tree, mild southern winds caressed the blushing rose in all her maiden bashfulness. The odors of the dew-lit chalice stole softly into the silent air of night, and in her burning chastity of passion the flower yielded all her sweet virginity. The leaves fell fading to the ground, and only stem and spine looked up to the blackest sky.

JESHUA. Life is to all a mournful dream.

ZENOBIA. Should I have thrown away the withered wreath which has ornamented my hair, hung my rumpled garment on the thorny hedge and donned a servant's garb?

JESHUA. I pity you.

ZENOBIA. No, I continue to drink the bacchanalian joys of life! I kindle the evanescent sparks of the hearth to a mighty flame, enrapture and drink enraptures, receive and give, think and feel with the ambitious energy of youth, though spring has left my features and the noonday sun has passed the summit. Follow me to fragrant bowers! The wrinkled garments fall from my limbs, while the languid, half-closed eyes look around in search. You, the lover, sink down at my side.

JESHUA. Temptress, leave me! I can never be yours!

ZENOBIA. Press closer and closer to me! Listen to nature's voice. It is the expression of our overflowing lives. The forests sound, the waters roar, and in the trembling air the fire flies build their heaven of sparkling light, like fickle stars that crowd the firmament of night.

JESHUA. Let me go! Inordinate love can gain no power over me.

ZENOBIA. Behold me as I am! [*Rends her garment.*] This godlike form is yours!

JESHUA [*yields for one moment, then suddenly frees himself*]. I still resist!

ZENOBIA. —What woman's son are you? —I see my

efforts to conquer you are in vain; but in my body boils a sea of blood. Now I give vent to all inhuman feelings that find shelter in my belly's flame! [*Seizes her dagger.*] I'll limb and laniate the body of my wayward suitor; lacerate his selfish heart, and amidst writhing mutilations and smoking sloughs of blood, I shall stand triumphant! [*Stands for one moment transfigured as the incarnation of lust, then throws herself upon* JESHUA, *who disarms and forces her to the ground. A groan comes from* ZENOBIA'S *lips, she murmurs.*] Forgive! [*And clings to the burning sand in voluptuous despair. The sun burns intensely.*]

JESHUA. Oh, woman, your incessant, fearful struggle of the body with the soul, of light with darkness, reality with the ideal, is like the universal song of life and death. You are immortal, even with your faults, which fetter you to the shadow of shadows, and your virtues, which lift you to the light of lights.

CURTAIN

ACT II

Scene III

SCENE: *As in Act I* JESHUA's *brothers and sisters, eating dried dates and drinking camel's milk, sit in the garden.* JESHUA *mends his Sabbath breeches.*

MAGDALEN. Brother, what is love?

JESHUA. A flower growing in the human soul. Its buds break forth and open to a life of sunshine. At first a zephyr gently kisses the trembling leaves; suddenly a storm starts up, and the chill, dark earth consumes its fading charms. For the flower of love has no abode on earth; her yearning is for an eternally faraway home, from whence she has come, to which she must return. And if she reveals herself in her serenest beauty, she stands on the grave of two human beings, who have drunk from her chalice the benediction of another world.

MAGDALEN. This is very sad; and does love never dwell upon earth in any other form?

JESHUA. Never.

MOTHER MARIA [*sings inside the cottage*]. Unhappy lovers, young widows and widowers, parents sitting at the empty cradle, beggars, all diseased and deformed beings, poets and artists without success,

Toil along, toil along!

[*Calls.*] Come in, my children. Leave Jeshua alone!

MAGDALEN. Never tell me such a story again, for it makes me weep. I feel as if the angels had to weep in heaven to see such sorrow upon earth. [*Opens her eyes wide, with an*

147

expression of innocence, as if her glance should penetrate all the world. Children exit.]

JESHUA. Who can understand the soul of children? —They should be taught by the young. —We will never get farther than this child—. What will my future Magdalen be? —Last night I beheld a world sublime beneath the sky; how can I speak such bitter words of sorrow now? [HANNAH *enters.*] Strange feelings have come over me. I hardly know myself. [*Breaks a lily and plucks out the stamens.*]

[*Pause.*]

BOTH [*as before*]. The chaos of our childlike dreams have merged into unsatisfied desires. Our love is poisoned by heart-corroding thoughts, and the mysteries of creation have become the temptation in our Eden-like dream. [*Their voices falter, tears fall from their eyes, profound sobs convulse their throats.* JESHUA *kneels at* HANNAH'S *feet, lowers his head in bitter supplication, and weeps. She looks at him with an expression of indescribable sadness, her whole body trembles, then the sunshine breaks through the clouds, an angelic smile glides over her face, and the drapery unveils itself from the divine beauty of her body. Music.* —HANNAH *hastily arranges her drapery, which formed a background to her denudation.*]

JESHUA. Your nakedness was a prayer! [*To* ELLOSAR, *who enters.*] Soon you will hear from me. The mission of my life begins this very hour. [MOTHER MARIA *enters the garden, and converses with* HANNAH.]

ELLOSAR. People, nowadays, believe only in signs and wonders.

JESHUA. Then I will stoop to do them.

ELLOSAR. Oh, that I could always stay with you!

JESHUA. You could forget yourself, but not your art.

ELLOSAR. Oh, my beloved art!

JESHUA. Fair for a day.

ELLOSAR. Fair for ages to come! Art eternizes whatever is beautiful; each idea by purity composed has right to breathe the vital air. Inspirations of color, sound, or thought will yet survive when the pyramids have fallen to ruins, and the temple of Jerusalem no longer lifts its golden dome against the azure of the timeless sky.

JESHUA. May be, but to what end?

ELLOSAR. To beautify—to beautify!

JESHUA. Proceed, my prophet, and with the crown of martyrdom enter the kingdom of heaven!

ELLOSAR. I wonder who is the greater dreamer of us two? [*Sits down near the well.*]

MAGDALEN [*enters*]. Brother, take a walk with me!

[JESHUA *takes her hand.*]

MOTHER MARIA. Bring me home some flowers.

MAGDALEN. I am not to break any flowers.

MOTHER MARIA. Why, my darling?

MAGDALEN. I think that flowers have a soul like human beings.

MOTHER MARIA. Angel, a flower yourself! [JESHUA *and* MAGDALEN *exit.*]

HANNAH. I love him more than God and all existences! Oh, Mother, do you know those moments when a soul in ecstasy of bliss rises to the eye in shape of tears, moments when our faltering lips would murmur words of wonder, what mighty incomprehensible thoughts the human mind can hide, which give us a glimpse into infinity which give us the right to hope?

MOTHER MARIA. I do, my child, only too well.

HANNAH. Thus I have felt since his first kiss which still glows upon my lips. If there is a Paradise on earth, it is this, it is this!

[TUBAL CAIN *passes by.*]

MOTHER MARIA. Your words return to me all that I have lost. God of my forefathers, send thy blessing upon these two until they find repose in thy omnipotence. [*Exits.*]

ELLOSAR [*watching* HANNAH, *aside*]. Oh, Jeshua, let thyself sink deep into the inward smile of loving souls.

HANNAH. If I could make him happy!

SADAKICHI HARTMANN

AHOLIBAH [*followed by* ZENOBIA, *disguised*].   Hasten, he may soon return.

ZENOBIA.   Leave me! [*Hands gold to* AHOLIBAH, *who joins* ELLOSAR.] I have arranged my plans. [*Laughs wildly.*] How that homely mendicant in patched clothes can make him dream of love! [*To* HANNAH.] Where are your thoughts?

HANNAH [*absent minded*].   With him, alas!

ZENOBIA.   You recognize me?

HANNAH [*nods*].   What do you want of him?

ZENOBIA.   Fear not that I come to do him injury.

HANNAH [*murmurs*].   He is invulnerable.

ZENOBIA.   I also love him.

HANNAH.   Who can help loving him? —How I pity you.

ZENOBIA [*aside*].   Audacious one! —You know the ambition of his life?

HANNAH.   I feel what it might be. He will succeed.

ZENOBIA [*aside*].   Oh, for her faith! And yet one obstacle exists.

HANNAH.   Name it.

ZENOBIA.   It would make you more unfortunate than human lips can devise.

HANNAH.   I do not understand. No service which I could render him would bring unhappiness to me. Name it, I implore you.

ZENOBIA.   He loves his ambition most of all. Your faithfulness would hinder him in its fulfillment.

[*Pause.*]

HANNAH.   That my dream should come to such an end! Life without him will be a void, for I loved him, not love.

ZENOBIA.   He loves love.

HANNAH.   I obey.

ZENOBIA.   Your self-denial will bear fruit, though you may never witness it.

HANNAH.   I will gladly bear all in his name, unworthy as I am. And now away, far away, over burning deserts!

150

ZENOBIA.   Remain with me in your distress. You shall be
my bosom friend, [*Aside.*] my slave!

HANNAH.   Lead me forth!

ZENOBIA.   We both will mourn for him. [*Aside.*] Now I
may hope for victory.

HANNAH.   Farewell, lord of my soul, farewell!

[*Exits with* ZENOBIA.]

AHOLIBAH.   Oh, Ellosar, you despise me because I like to
be caressed and kissed by those I love. Does not the bee also
prefer to suck the thyme because it gives the sweetest
honey? Am I so different to other girls? Show me one who
does not go astray before her marriage.

[OTHNIEL *and* REUBEN, EVA *and* TABEA *enter.*]

ELLOSAR.   No embroidered garments, however flaunting
they may be, can hide the leprous sores of vice. And many a
female, though virgin-knotted still, may be a greater harlot
than she who is the odious friend of every man.

AHOLIBAH.   You are cruel and unjust. How can a woman
remain pure. Has nature fashioned her to live an abstemious
life? Women have, perhaps, more right to expect chastity of
men, than you of us.

ELLOSAR.   I bear you no ill. Yet some night when your
hands are toying with your breasts, or glide listlessly
between your thighs, make an effort, stop your wilful play,
and ponder on maternity.

OTHNIEL.   Who knows how you will speak thirty years
hence? Perhaps like bald-pated Habakuk around the corner,
who did not succeed in reforming the world, and now is
doing trade in bread and cheese. He grumbles, "Fine arts
are very nice; but to make money in this damned country
one has to sell something that turns into dung."

ELLOSAR.   A person who listens to a dirty story without
disgust, should be spit at.

OTHNIEL [*laughs*].   You better change humanity into a
spitting dish, moral philosopher!

151

ELLOSAR. What is the use of art for Othniels? My consolation is that every human being is of some use. So also my efforts will not be in vain. Should I die unknown they will be like the blossoms which the trees shake off in spring; if I succeed, like those who defy the threatening siege of rain and storm, and finally bear fruit.

TUBAL CAIN [*enters and* MOTHER MARIA, *standing at the door, leaves on perceiving him*]. She does not wish to see me. Well, Mother Maria, I will get there after all. If it could only be done without wooing. Why not simply say, I am male, you are female—let us marry; let us have offspring. The animals have more sense than we.

[HAGAR *and other girls come home singing from the fields.*]

TABEA. A weird song!

EVA [*dressed in dark blue, with red girdle and red blossoms in her hair*]. Like the curious question, What comes after death?

ELLOSAR. Look at these flowers, just gathered from the field. How beautiful they are! What fragrant smell! Now, look at these that fade away. O'er what regions do their odors roam? Your answer tells what human minds of immortality may know.

OTHNIEL. What a wonderful imagination!

REUBEN [*shaking his head*]. Onanism!

OTHNIEL. A peculiar association of ideas!

REUBEN. Why, human beings are after all nothing but degenerated animals, degenerated by mental self-abuse.

OTHNIEL. I believe you would make an owl of your mother, if it would serve your argument.

REUBEN. Why not, as long as I am in the right?

TABEA. I fear nobody exactly knows what is right or wrong.

REUBEN. Right is where conviction is.

ELLOSAR. Then everyone is right, and all controversy ends.

152

OTHNIEL. No generation is ripe for the revelation of two geniuses.

ELLOSAR. Tabea hinted at the truth. One human being never learns to understand another; even parents and children, brothers and sisters, husbands and wives walk side by side, like perfect strangers, through this life.

TUBAL CAIN. And well for them that it is so. How could a man succeed otherwise?

OTHNIEL. I am sure you have grown fat by the ignorance of others.

REUBEN. Nature gave him cupidity, and he made use of it.

TABEA. Could not success spring from a purer source?

ELLOSAR. It often does, but the waters grow turbid as they onward flow.

TUBAL CAIN. Every word you speak is dirt; he, he. A man succeeds only by patience, cunning, and hard labor. In the beginning be a sycophant, adnescent to every one you need. Sell your conscience, turn a hypocrite, pry for the weakness of superiors, seize every opportunity by which to rise, and by persistent knavery—clandestine, of course—success is sure to come. Then kick aside superfluous friends, and profit by your slyness. Be a blood-sucker, incendiary, virgin violator, the most infamous wretch that ever breathed, all the same they'll come and lick your feet. Believe old Tubal Cain; he may be wrong in many things, but he is right in this. Now for a flask of wine with Habakuk!

[*Exits;* OTHNIEL, REUBEN, *and* TABEA *follow.*]

HAGAR. I understand nothing of their talk. I work the whole day in the fields, and when I come home I take care of my younger sisters and brothers. I have not even time to pray. I am happy only when I am asleep. A terrible guilt must rest upon us that we can be so unhappy. [*Slowly exits.*]

ELLOSAR [*watching* EVA]. For ages could I look at her

153

latent, luscious limbs. Each of her motions reveals the sumptuous sensuousness of all terrestrial scenes. The fiery flame of twilight gold on her white marble limbs, the distant blue, the pink and green suggestions, mysterious tints, sighs of virginity, sweet music to the eye! Her arms, her heaving breast, the chaste line of her tender, swelling hips, the night of ebon hair. And then her lap, night within light, dark star of future's hope, the unattainable of vital strength—creative beauty, sempiternal, forming the uniting link between man and the infinite! An angel lost between heaven and earth, the light of god upon her head and her feet wrapt in the shadow of fleeting days! [*Joins* EVA *at the well.*] Will you share this drink with me?

EVA [*looks dreamfully at him, then drinks*]. Oh, if it were the draught of oblivion! [*A heavenly smile plays around* ELLOSAR'S *lips; he presses a kiss on her sad, dark eyes, her pale cheeks begin to glow, a warm, melodious mystery quivers through every atom of her soul.*]

[*Long pause.*]

EVA. My love died without the crowning glory of a woman's fate. A life-long ache in a nightless life has sealed the surrender of my yesterdays.

[*Pause.*]

ELLOSAR. Eva, confide in me! The secret, long-sorrowing of your soul is sacred to me. Oh, do not blush! You have loved, but in vain. You are childless against your will. Be not ashamed! I am as healthy in body and mind as you. One fierce embrace suffices. The *idea* alone shall reign when we are linked together. Take this kiss unto the welfare of the child which now we shall create. [*He kisses her forehead, leading her away.*] Come, lie with me, muse of my body! Uncover your nakedness! Let flesh be flesh, let soul be soul! Perfume of maternity, rise into the air! We create our children, not in tepid chambers with lurking sensations in the regions of shame, nor on debauchment's bed of flowers of soft, sirenic power, but undraped in the open air, on the life-kindling bosom of mother earth. The philistines will cry: "The land has fallen to abomination!" The prophets of mankind will murmur: "The dawn of another race!"

[*Exits with* EVA.]

JESHUA [*enters, carrying* MAGDALEN *in his arms; he carries her into the cottage; re-enters, and stands at the garden gate*]. An unredeemable dreariness of thought has come over me. I have a strange presentiment that something terrible will happen before the close of this day. Where is Hannah? I see her nowhere. Hannah! Hannah! No answer! Where can she be?

AHOLIBAH [*timidly, having remained in the background during the preceding scenes*].   I know where Hannah is.

JESHUA.   Speak!

AHOLIBAH.   She has left the village, with the foreign queen.

JESHUA [*utters a cry of despair, and falls backwards; his mother and a few passing friends gather around him. It grows dark, as before a coming storm. He rises suddenly*].   Follow me!

CURTAIN

ACT III

SCENE: *Camp in the desert. Before a tent, to the right,* ZENOBIA, *crowned and in gold and crimson drapery, rests on a couch, like a personification of the world's agony, attended by* CAMILLUS *and* PARSONDES. *An orgy, magnificent and unrestrained, occupies the remainder of the stage. A feast of colors, as suggested in the pictures of Hans Makart, pervades the scene. In the background, a group of palm trees, behind it a view on the desert.* HANNAH *is seen among a group of slaves.*

ZENOBIA. Oh, voluptuous breath of life, burst from the intestines of the earth, and overwhelm me in thy furious majesty! Simoons, come from the desert, devour me in your burning heat! I can no longer breathe in this dark solitude. Pent-up rivers, descend in torrents, embrace me with your foaming waves, and carry me back to the watery chaos! Oh, glowing fires above my head, fall from heaven and burn these mighty limbs to ashes!

There is a fire in my breast! Bring me some palm-wine! Some wine, I say! [*Tears the goblet with a threatening gesture from the slave, empties it in one gulp, and hurls it to the ground; to the slave.*] Ha! you are strong and nobly built. —Take him away! My Lybian lions roar for food. Strike the cymbals, eat and drink, glorify my divinity!

Life glares at me like the empty black bottomless eye-sockets of my punished slaves. The god of this land separated light from darkness, why not in me? When will the sun break through the storm-cloud of my sorrow? A ghost of barrenness is doomed forever to haunt the labyrinth be-

156

neath these fervid breasts. I have given orders that the poems of Sappho should be demolished, and my golden verses distributed instead. I have sent hundreds of sculptors to Mount Sinai to change that mountain into one mighty, colossal bust of me. I shall have temples erected all over this floating sphere, and everyone shall mock at the Ephesians' arrogance. All this, however, leaves the same frost and fire within me. Oh, had I the power to chain the tempests, and move the mountains at my command! Oh, had I a thousand bodies that I could lie with a thousand kings at one mad moment of inebriation! Oh, were the ocean a goblet of blood, that I could gulp it down in one draught! Would that satisfy me? —No!

Where are my stewards, Camillus, Koa, and the rest? Gold, gold, more gold, I cry! [*Scatters gold.*] I want a hundredfold Croesean wealth to build a road to heaven, that I may visit unknown worlds.

What are these fireballs that dance before my eyes? These grinning faces—myriads of faces! Now they unite into one Cyclopean head, with the same abominable grin around its haggard lips. Hand me a flaming sword! I'll chop it off from the misshapen shoulders of the universe, that I may be alone with myself and the eternity of my despair. This world is too narrow for more than one. —I am queen of earth, lady of heaven, mother of all existences! Kneel and tremble! [*Her vassals kneel.*] Kill me, gods, or I'll kill you! [*Stares motionless at heaven.*] There is a blot upon my brain, and I see life in different colors to the rest. What power has a god? Can they forget the past? No, even the deathless gods are deprived of making that which is past, undone. [*Aside, showing her teeth.*] All this is but a vulgar comedy, and I play the fool myself. [*To the stewards.*] Distribute some precious stones among my guests—sapphires, as hard as they. [*To* CAMILLUS.] Let your hand rest upon my forehead, Camillus. All seem satisfied, save I.

CAMILLUS. My queen, a passion like yours will never be understood.

ZENOBIA. What shall I do?

CAMILLUS. How can a mortal counsel god?

ZENOBIA. There must be something which could radiate the empty void around the earth, within my soul.

CAMILLUS. To squander love, and ask for no return.

ZENOBIA. To squander love, and ask for no return would be the birthday of another life. Yet I cannot stand at the portals of glory and bestow such benevolence. My world-wide passion yells for sempiternal sin.

Oh, Tammuz, why didst thou betray me? At thy breast of fire I would never have felt the power of darkness which now pervades my life. Love is the light which illumines all, and once extinguished nothing remains but perdition. Oh, Tammuz, return with thy purple flood of light; let me sink into thy languid stream of gold; let me dissolve in thy glorious heat—lost, lost forever!

CAMILLUS Alas! who has not experienced the pangs of love?

ZENOBIA. You also, Camillus?

CAMILLUS. Yes, my queen. I also roamed through the garden of Aphrodite, dreaming that its roads were strewn with roses, sonnets, and laurel crowns. The brilliant skies have lost their brightness. We left those beautiful shores of golden sand, and the waves which caressed the sea shells on the strand have lost their crest of silver foam. We have departed from that island, with its verdant hills. The melancholy dreams of future bliss no longer visit us in the sylvan groves of hope, and the roads, where we wandered arm in arm, are desolate, overgrown with weeds, like lonesome walks in the historical gardens of the past. Only the marble temple of our love still stands in all its majesty, amidst the changing scenes of autumn, but the fire of its altar is long extinguished, and the garlands of luminous

158

flowers which entwined the columns have long withered, and only the sweet sadness of our childish faith still lingers in that realm of peace. At times, dreamlike melodies carry me back to the classic shores of Greece, where the human body in all its naked purity, sculptures lines of poetry into the marble blocks of Paros. Oh, could I wander again along the villas near the sea, and there under the dark foliage of the cypress trees, while yellow leaves sweep over marble steps, dream the dreams of a happy past.

PARSONDES. Zenobia, so deep in thought?

ZENOBIA. And you shouting for pleasure as loud as ever?

PARSONDES. That alone is joy in living! To dress in the finest shades of green and blue; to carry a sharp sword; to bridle a fire-striking mare; to be wasteful to excess in drink and food! To force some cold, bright beauty to the ground, to carnalize a stubborn, struggling sacrifice, while strained eyeballs and meandering tongue still indicate desires indomitable! Let me unkiss the wanton sorrow between your lips incarnadine!

ZENOBIA. Camillus, something to while away the time.

CAMILLUS. My queen? A fight of female gladiators—the rites of violation—a sanguinarian tragedy—the dithyrambs of northern bards—Atma, the dancing woman.

ZENOBIA. Let her appear!

[ATMA, *of lush and lithsome shape, draped in silvery gauze, veiling her as water veils a bather, enters. Her loose, dark hair is interwoven with golden threads. Her saint-like visage, with its deep, sad eyes, bears Pre-Raphaelitic reminiscences. She stretches her limbs in full enjoyment of life, and endeavors to express by the most rhythmical motions, accompanied by soft music, all phases of love. Beginning with the purely physical, her dance becomes more and more dignified and spiritualized until at last it represents the ecstasy of perfect purity in love. Her limbs reveal the highest poetic beauty capable of being expressed by the human*

*body, and Dancing reaches in this new, ideal way of revealing
abstract beauty, the glory of her arts.*]

CAMILLUS. What suggestions for an artist! What inspiration for a poet's soul! What ethereal flights towards the infinite!

ZENOBIA [*to* ATMA]. Take this tiara!

PARSONDES. How, my love's oblation!

ZENOBIA [*to* ATMA]. Be free! You gave me for one moment oblivion of myself.

CAMILLUS. That woman has driven all repose from my breast. The Lydian dreams of her marble limbs make me tremble. The Greek statues are awakened to musical life. A new art has risen from the past.

PARSONDES. And all this you see in that lean woman over there?

CAMILLUS. I do. Form-language seems to be incomprehensible to you; there are but few who understand it.

PARSONDES [*shrugs his shoulders*]. Zenobia, the night is cool and it grows late. The waters deluged the red Nelumbus long ago. Oblivion from the hungry, idle monotony of day beckons from yonder tent, and where the giant tiger skin is spread, let your lyre sound the song of love's great rage; let me, like night upon the darkening world, descend upon your trembling, glowing frame.

ZENOBIA. It would not tremble nor glow for you. Hours of unknown joys soar from my darksome bed, and luxuries unseen, unfelt, obliviate my tremulent past. The sea of lust recedes, and the sound of the softest kiss sojourns in sylvan scenes, where the nightingale is sweetly singing, where brisk morning breezes sway, and where the bee is humming from flower to flower.

PARSONDES. Fluid sighs and weaving pain—golden cataracts bursting through love's domain—all creation sinks low as the waters glow, as we absorb the scaturient flow— deep, darkling desires—fire in fire—daedalian coition— antemundane nihilation— [*Seizes her with violence.*]

160

ZENOBIA. Begone! Take away your wanton face; all vices of humanity cry from your earth-drawn limbs! One step nearer, and this dagger will be plunged into your venomous breast!

PARSONDES [*staggering, hisses forth*]. Your immane pride shall have its fall, poor, wasted, aging godling! I cease to be your paramour. In amorous fever search in vain for other kings of ideal adulation—while I in wild delight, roam night for night through variegated fields of fornication! Women serving but as drains for men are indistinguishable to me. [*To partakers of the bacchanal.*] Fair hoiden, come! [*Gropes at her lactescent bosom.*] or your flesh in venerous heat will burst through its pregnant vesture tonight. And you, dumb statue of maidenhood demure, I swear your cold carnation will yet be inflamed, that like Zuleikha's glossy skin, it will be irradiant of all carnal sin. Come all, undrape, nudate, and in amorous confusion form Prince Parsondes' cushion, cover, and couch! [*The courtezans shrink before him in sexual disgust or hope, as they accompany him.*]

ZENOBIA [*to the rest*]. Leave me!

CAMILLUS. Good night, fair queen. May your heart be at rest, may the gods grant you extended years of glory! [*Exit.*]

ZENOBIA. The present is born in agony and sinks with agony into the past. Night and day pass each other in dreadful silence, and stare into my despairing face. What pleasures have been floating down on my rapid stream of life? Its rushing torrents brought me nothing but desire, brutal acts, and then disgust. And now, having met the man who could change my whole existence, in repugnant pity he turns from me, despises me for her, this beggar-child [*Seizes her lyre, and sings softly.*]

When gardens lie dreaming in moonlight, the nocturnal flower begins her reign, unfastening her mantle of glimmering white, perfuming the air with a sinful strain.

The night moths are lured to the dangerous fire, each sips from the nectar of her desire, while her soul is yearning for

161

unknown treasures that can never be hers in her life of pleasures.

[*It grows silent in the camp. The cries of hyenas now and then interrupt the stillness.*]

Oh, night, send a mild and balmy influence o'er my frame! The sins I have committed turn to righteousness in the restless sable clouds of thy mysterious power. Lull my thoughts into quiescence; lowery darkness loom before my lurid inward eye, and give me sleep—sleep—death!

Death? Death is my bitterest foe! Dreadful vision of decay, do not grind thy yellow, jagged teeth at me; drag thee aside, or my fist will break thy monstrous gaping jaw of black, unfathomable mystery! There it comes crawling towards me, and rolls its eyes in furious rage. Its pointed, winding tongue jerks for my breasts. Its boiling, putrid breath stagnates the air. Diseased claws dig deep and deeper into my angry flesh. Help, help! I will depopulate the world, and feed you with its carcasses. Gnaw away my outward beauty; let me rot, but let me live! Strike me blind, deaf, dumb, immovable, and I will thank thee still, if you but let me live! I beg thee, I command thee, let me live! Who is there? [*Runs up to* HANNAH, *who enters.*] Ah! it is you—through whom I suffer. By what magic did you win his love? Confess, or I will kill you.

HANNAH. I loved him, and he—loved me.

ZENOBIA. What else?

HANNAH. I know not.

ZENOBIA. You lie! [*Strikes her.*]

HANNAH. I forgive you.

ZENOBIA. Speak!

HANNAH. Strike me again.

ZENOBIA. You refuse? Then you must die.

HANNAH. May it be so.

ZENOBIA [*claps her hands.* CAMILLUS *enters*]. Strike off her head, and hurl it into some hyena's jaw.

162

CAMILLUS. I cannot.

ZENOBIA. Do it, or suffer death yourself.

CAMILLUS. I cannot.

ZENOBIA. I'll do it myself! —I cannot. [*Sits down. An attendant enters in haste, and whispers to* CAMILLUS.]

CAMILLUS. My queen, the young Jew stands at the entrance of the camp, and asks admittance.

ZENOBIA [*takes a deep breath*]. Is he alone?

CAMILLUS. No, a tall Jewish woman stands at his side, and a few friends accompany him.

ZENOBIA. If you value your life, let them not enter! [CAMILLUS *exits.*] What will the coming hour reveal to me?

HANNAH. He calls me. I hear it, and I must welcome him.

ZENOBIA [*aside*]. Now I must venture all; now or never. His she shall not be at any cost! How now, Camillus?

CAMILLUS [*enters*]. He has entered.

ZENOBIA. Have I no body guard? Are my servants all asleep? They shall suffer for it, and so shall you, ungrateful hound!

CAMILLUS. The guards are as blameless as I. Nobody can use violence if the earnest, piercing glance of that young Jew is fastened upon one's face.

ZENOBIA [*looks at a ring on her finger, which contains poison, seizes a goblet, puts the poison into the drink*]. Hannah, your lover has come, and you shall follow him. Come, drink with me to his happy return!

HANNAH [*drinks*]. Jehovah be praised for his wonderful guidance that led Jeshua back to my arms!

CAMILLUS. My queen, they come. [JESHUA *enters, followed by* MOTHER MARIA, ELLOSAR, AHOLIBAH, *and a few villagers.*]

JESHUA. Queen, return my love to me.

ZENOBIA. Take her, there she stands.

[HANNAH *bursts forth with a cry of joy. Enraptured she*

163

throws her arms wide open, makes a few steps towards JESHUA, *then staggers and faints away.*]

JESHUA.   Hannah, what has befallen you? Speak, look up, your love has come, and waits for you. Hannah, awake! Open your eyes, and speak to me! No answer. Your hands are of eburnean hue, your limbs are stiff and lifeless. Could it be? [*To* CAMILLUS.] Speak, if you know! Is she dead?

CAMILLUS [*firmly*].   She is poisoned.

JESHUA [*stands for a moment, as if petrified, then makes a sign to his mother and friends to be calm*].   Peace! Be still! She speaks.

HANNAH.   Let me fall into slumber. It is better so. I had nothing to do in this world but to make you happy, and for that you are not in need of me. I do not wish to darken the splendor of the sun. Do not mourn for me, yet think of me often when I am no more. Farewell, beloved, farewell! Is it the last farewell?

[*She looks for a long while up to heaven, then turns her eyes on* JESHUA, *and dies.*]

MOTHER MARIA.   Woman, restore her life, or I will strangle thee with these, a mother's hands. Do you hear me?

ZENOBIA [*absentminded*].   I see but him. Who are you?

MOTHER MARIA.   His mother, who will avenge her death, if such a crime can be avenged.

JESHUA.   Mother, use no violence; you have no right to do so.

MOTHER MARIA.   How! No retribution?

JESHUA.   No, Mother no. [*To the others.*] Respect the dead!

MOTHER MARIA.   Maranatha! Maranatha! —Oh, that that demon could feel no pity for this tender flower!

JESHUA.   Yes, Hannah, thou art like a broken flower. Thus far thou couldst blossom in this garden of transitoriness, now bloom on over the grave! The beautiful has no abode on earth.

[AHOLIBAH, *in mute despair, draws close her robe over her breasts.*]

ELLOSAR [*aside*]. Oh, Jeshua, the fire of your soul is so prolific that every spark will kindle conflagrations in countless lives of countless generations!

ZENOBIA [*lost in wonder, steps to* JESHUA, *kneels at his feet, her head bent low. He takes her head between his hands, and looks with sublime sadness into her eyes. An idea of immortality begins to dawn upon* ZENOBIA's *mind. She speaks in a trembling voice*]. Master, judge your slave!

JESHUA. I have no right to judge. We all are sinners, and need salvation. Let the god of truth forgive us all! [*In an undertone.*] All forgiving love is the redemption of my faith.

[*For the first time a halo is seen around* JESHUA's *head, caused by a concentration of light on his back. All kneel or bow their heads in reverence.*]

CURTAIN

165

Suggestions for a Performance of "Christ"

In case the author could not be present to supervise the first production of his drama "Christ," the following demands are made by him, the fulfillment of which he deems not only desirable, but essential for a satisfactory performance:

1. A well-ventilated theatre, with comfortable seats, each commanding a perfect view of the whole stage.

2. An intelligent audience, not indulging in the naughty caprice of coming too late, of leaving their seats regularly during the intermission, of wearing colossal hats, of chatting and laughing during the performance, and of applauding at the most inappropriate occasions.

3. An invisible orchestra of first-class musicians (the dramatic music to be descriptive in the style of Massenet).

4. A proscenium enclosed by a large, broad, golden frame, so that every situation on the stage is made to appear like the representation of a painting, and that from curtain to curtain the action proceeds like a series of pictures, each worthy of a painter of repute.

5. A stage manager who, in his directions and arrangements, will borrow freely from all arts, and prove bold enough to gain a laurel wreath in introducing successfully the nude into the dramatic art. (If he should grow a little nervous at the "undrape" of Hannah and Zenobia, and the orgy in the camp, he is kindly asked to remember that tact and bold artistic inspiration will overcome all obstacles.)

6. Actors and actresses who are not exclusively merce-

166

nary in their views, and believe that the dramatic art has other ends besides that of amusing. (The author would like to see a Duse or Clara Morris as Aholibah, a Possart or Got as Tubal Cain.)

7. Supernumeraries, superior to those of the Saxe-Meiningen Company, i.e., who are more natural and artistic, by displaying a greater variety of movement and expression, without becoming conspicuous.

8. Light and atmospheric effects as perfect as contemporary science, skill, and taste can produce (for instance an adaptation of those used at the Urania lectures).

9. Panorama-like scenery, with effects of impressionism always in harmony with costumes and accessories.

10. Costumes revealing a close study of the innumerable pictures that relate to the Old and New Testaments.

11. Picturesque and natural looking, if necessary, solid properties.